Spoiler Groups and UN Peacekeeping

Peter Nadin

Patrick Cammaert

Vesselin Popovski

Spoiler Groups and UN Peacekeeping

Peter Nadin

Patrick Cammaert

Vesselin Popovski

IISS The International Institute for Strategic Studies

The International Institute for Strategic Studies

Arundel House | 13–15 Arundel Street | Temple Place | London | WC2R 3DX | UK

First published February 2015 **Routledge**
4 Park Square, Milton Park, Abingdon, Oxon, OX14 4RN

for **The International Institute for Strategic Studies**
Arundel House, 13–15 Arundel Street, Temple Place, London, WC2R 3DX, UK
www.iiss.org

Simultaneously published in the USA and Canada by **Routledge**
270 Madison Ave., New York, NY 10016

Routledge is an imprint of Taylor & Francis, an Informa Business

DIRECTOR-GENERAL AND CHIEF EXECUTIVE Dr John Chipman
EDITOR Dr Nicholas Redman
EDITORIAL MANAGER Nancy Turner
EDITORIAL Mona Moussavi, Jill Lally, Anna Ashton
COVER/PRODUCTION John Buck, Kelly Verity

The International Institute for Strategic Studies is an independent centre for research, information and debate on the problems of conflict, however caused, that have, or potentially have, an important military content. The Council and Staff of the Institute are international and its membership is drawn from almost 100 countries. The Institute is independent and it alone decides what activities to conduct. It owes no allegiance to any government, any group of governments or any political or other organisation. The IISS stresses rigorous research with a forward-looking policy orientation and places particular emphasis on bringing new perspectives to the strategic debate.

The Institute's publications are designed to meet the needs of a wider audience than its own membership and are available on subscription, by mail order and in good bookshops. Further details at www.iiss.org.

Printed and bound in Great Britain by Bell & Bain Ltd, Thornliebank, Glasgow

British Library Cataloguing in Publication Data
A catalogue record for this book is available from the British Library

Library of Congress Cataloging in Publication Data

ADELPHI series
ISSN 1944-5571

ADELPHI 449
ISBN 978-1-138-92496-3

Contents

ACKNOWLEDGEMENTS

I would like to thank my co-authors Patrick Cammaert and Vesselin Popo-vski. General Cammaert led a distinguished career as a UN peacekeeping commander in Ethiopia–Eritrea (UNMEE) and the Democratic Republic of the Congo (MONUC). When he speaks about peacekeeping he speaks from experience, he speaks with passion. When I invited him to join me in writing this book, he could have so easily declined the offer. Instead, Patrick engaged with the project. He took time out of his busy schedule to help develop the key concepts contained therein. I thank him for his work and commitment. I would also like to thank Vesselin Popovski for his enormous support through the entire process of writing this book. His contribution and guidance have been invaluable.

I must also extend a word of thanks to the people I have met along this journey. I extend a word of thanks to those interviewees who gave so generously of their time and provided such useful insights: Ian Martin, Jean-Marie Guéhenno, Colonel Michael Redman, Major-General Adrian Foster, Lieutenant-General Abhijit Guha, Ian Sinclair, François Grignon, Methil Siva, and Connie Peck. I would also like to thank L. Murray McCullough. He helped me enormously while I was based in New York in the SSR unit, DPKO. He shared his wisdom, acted as a sounding board and organised interviews.

I wish to thank the International Institute for Strategic Studies (IISS) for granting us the opportunity to write this book. Two people at IISS deserve a special word of thanks. Firstly, Nick Redman, editor of the *Adelphi* series, for shepherding me through the entire 18-month process – from proposal to publication. Secondly, Mona Moussavi, our wonderful editor, for setting aside her studies to edit the manuscript. We owe both Nick and Mona a debt of gratitude for their work.

Peter Nadin

LIST OF UN ACRONYMS AND ABBREVIATIONS

DPA	Department of Political Affairs
DPKO	Department of Peacekeeping Operations
FIB	Force Intervention Brigade
JMAC	Joint Mission Analysis Centre
JOC	Joint Operations Centre
MINURCAT	United Nations Mission in the Central African Republic and Chad
MINUSCA	United Nations Multidimensional Integrated Stabilisation Mission in the Central Africa Republic
MINUSMA	United Nations Multidimensional Stabilisation Mission in Mali
MONUC	United Nations Organisation Mission in the Democratic Republic of the Congo
MONUSCO	United Nations Organisation Stabilisation Mission in the Democratic Republic of the Congo
SRSG	Special Representative of the Secretary-General
UNAMET	United Nations Assistance Mission in East Timor
UNAMID	United Nations African Union Hybrid Mission in Darfur
UNAMIR	United Nations Assistance Mission in Rwanda
UNAMSIL	United Nations Mission in Sierra Leone
UNITAF	United Task Force (Somalia)
UNMISS	United Nations Mission in South Sudan
UNOSOM I/II/II	United Nations Operation in Somalia (I/II/III)
UNPROFOR	United Nations Protection Force
UNTAES	United Nations Transitional Administration for Eastern Slavonia, Baranja and Western Sirmium
UNTAET	United Nations Transitional Administration in East Timor

LIST OF OTHER ACRONYMS AND ABBREVIATIONS

ATT	Arms Trade Treaty
C2	Command and Control
CAR	Central African Republic
DDR	Disarmament, Demobilisation and Reintegration
DDRRR	Disarmament, Demobilisation, Repatriation, Reintegration and Resettlement
DPA	Darfur Peace Agreement
DRC	Democratic Republic of the Congo
ECOMOG	Economic Community of West African States Monitoring Group
ECOWAS	Economic Community of West African States
EUFOR Artemis	European Union Force Artemis (for the Ituri region of the DRC)
FARDC	Armed Forces of the Democratic Republic of the Congo
FOM	Freedom of Movement
G2	Division Level Intelligence
GoS	Government of Sudan
ICD	Inter-Congolese Dialogue
INTERFET	International Force for East Timor
ISAF	International Security Assistance Force (Afghanistan)
MNF	Multinational Force
POC	Protection of Civilians
ROE	Rules of Engagement
RRF	Rapid Reaction Force
SSR	Security Sector Reform

LIST OF ACRONYMS OF ARMED GROUPS

ACPLS	Alliance of Patriots for a Free and Sovereign Congo
ADF-Nalu	Allied Democratic Forces-Nalu
APC	All People's Congress
AQIM	Al-Qaeda in the Islamic Maghreb
CNDP	National Congress for the Defence of the People (Congrès national pour la défense du peuple)
CPJP	Convention of Patriots for Justice and Peace (Convention des Patriotes pour la Justice et la Paix)
CPSK	Patriotic Convention for the Salvation of Kodro (Convention Patriotique du salut du Kodro)
DLF	Darfur Liberation Front
FDLR	Democratic Forces for the Liberation of Rwanda
FMLN	Farabundo Martí National Liberation Front (Frente Farabundo Martí para la Liberación Nacional)
FNI	Nationalist and Integrationist Front
FRELIMO	Mozambique Liberation Front (Frente de Libertação de Moçambique)
IRA	Irish Republican Army
JEM	Justice and Equality Movement
LRA	Lord's Resistance Army
M23	March 23 Movement
MLC	Movement for the Liberation of Congo
MNLA	National Movement for the Liberation of Azawad (Mouvement National pour la Libération de l'Azawad)
NPFL	National Patriotic Front of Liberia

NWA   Nuer White Army

PARECO   Alliance of Resistant Congolese Patriots (Coalition des patriotes résistants congolais)

PIP   Postes d'intervention populaire

RCD-Goma   Rally for Congolese Democracy – Goma

RCD-ML   Rally for Congolese Democracy – Movement for Liberation

RCD-N   Rally for Congolese Democracy – National

RENAMO   Mozambican National Resistance (Resistência Nacional Moçambicana)

RUF   Revolutionary United Front

SLM/A   Sudan Liberation Movement/Army

SNM   Somali National Movement

SSDF   Somali Salvation Democratic Front

SWAPO   South West Africa People's Organization

UFDR   Union of Democratic Forces for Unity

UFR   Union of Republican Forces

UNITA   National Union for the Total Independence of Angola

USC   United Somali Congress

INTRODUCTION

Since the end of the Cold War, a marked shift in the nature of conflict and international politics has been witnessed. Both the proliferation and diversification of armed groups are, in large part, responsible for this shift. In an increasingly connected world, which advantages non-state actors, the centrality and power of the state is weakening. Conflicts continue to be fermented under the conditions of divisive patronage and identity politics, the unequal distribution of political and economic power, resource scarcity and widespread marginalisation coupled with disenfranchisement. These types of conflicts are marked by constant rebellion, the existence of 'dark networks'[1] and criminal agendas.

The ready availability of weapons and the emergence of new technologies have provided armed groups with the capacity to more effectively challenge the state. Street gangs, paramilitary forces, civil-defence groups, organised criminal networks, traffickers, bandits, warlords, militias and rebel splinter groups all have learnt to thrive in the stateless voids of hinterlands, borderlands, badlands and feral cities. Fuelled by both greed and grievance, they contest lax government authority, compete to control populations and actively seek to secure scarce resources. They can also be savagely brutal and unyielding in their defence of kin and brethren, yet astute in their provision of public goods through alternative systems of governance.

Both during and after civil war, non-state armed groups perform pivotal roles in shaping the battlespace, security situation and eventual peace. Following the end of conflict and the formalisation of a peace agreement, many groups accept the terms of the agreement and their members disarm, demobilise and reintegrate (DDR) back into society. Other groups, however, readily position themselves against the efforts of the international 'custodians of the peace'[2] (usually UN missions) and transitional governmental arrangements, in a bid to spoil any peace that does not accord with their interests. The term 'spoiler', coined by Stephen Stedman, is now a tag commonly applied to such groups. As keepers of the peace in many parts of the world, UN peacekeeping missions regularly confront spoilers with myriad motivations. Some groups are unsophisticated and rife with internal divisions, while others are adaptable, well connected and transnational. There are those that seek to turn a profit, while others seek to protect their communities.

With this in mind, how do UN missions engage with armed groups, and how can this engagement be improved? These are the questions at the heart of this *Adelphi* book.

UN missions

Since the new wave of UN peacekeeping began in 1999, UN missions have increasingly been mandated by the UN Security Council to eke out meagre gains in complex frontier environments – such as Darfur, South Sudan, the Democratic Republic of the Congo (DRC), Mali and West Africa. The job of UN missions has been to buttress fragile political agreements, consolidate state authority through a period of transition and, if all else fails, provide a modicum of protection for threatened civilians. In short, UN missions are tasked with the 'cultivation and protection of peace and the management of spoilers'.3 Considering the nature of these tasks, it is not unreasonable to argue that the success of UN missions is largely determined by how effectively they handle the challenges and opportunities presented by armed groups.

On an almost daily basis, the Security Council, the individual heads of mission (SRSGs) and, at the end of the chain, the peacekeeper on foot patrol are all confronted with a series of choices on how to handle armed spoilers: to deter, to assert, to neutralise (i.e. destroy), to pursue dialogue or to defer action. Interactions with armed groups, however, have been clouded by the UN's systemic bias towards the defence of the state. The UN is an organisation of member states, and UN missions are accordingly mandated to extend and consolidate state authority. This approach tends to position UN missions on the side of the government, and it is from this position that they choose how to address armed groups.

The leaders of UN missions can decide whether to co-opt or cajole armed groups into a peace or negotiated disarmament by means of effective mediation and the management of the country-specific political process. Of course, some spoilers virulently reject negotiations, and continue to pursue war-driven agendas. Inevitably, at this juncture, each UN mission is drawn into considering the use of force. On the far end of the spectrum, a UN mission may decide to designate an enemy and engage in military action to defeat that enemy – a position tantamount to war. A UN mission undertaking peace enforcement of this nature abandons impartiality and the principle of minimum use of force, and becomes a party to the conflict. As has been witnessed recently in the DRC, missions have been shown to naturally inch towards peace enforcement, if they are unable to make headway by other means. Mission creep owes much to a pent-up frustration and impatience with a mission's progress, and a desire to 'create military realities on the ground that would, in theory at any rate, facilitate the search for more lasting political solutions to the conflict at hand'.[4]

Conceptually and operationally, UN peacekeeping has been grappling with questions of force since the failures of the 1990s. In the organisational catharsis that followed, robust peacekeeping emerged as a potential new approach. Although still rather ambiguously defined, robust peacekeeping is often set against the concept of peace enforcement; while the latter entails the use of force at a strategic level, robust peacekeeping allows for force to be utilised only on a tactical level, as the Capstone Doctrine explains:

> The ultimate aim of the use of force is to influence and deter spoilers working against the peace process or seeking to harm civilians; and not to seek their military defeat. The use of force by a United Nations peacekeeping operation should always be calibrated in a precise, proportional and appropriate manner … in its use of force, a United Nations peacekeeping operation should always be mindful of the need for an early de-escalation of violence and a return to non-violent means of persuasion.[5]

The application of the concept has varied from mission to mission, as decisions around the use of force have remained flexible and based on real-time assessments of SRSGs, force commanders and contingent commanders influenced by instructions from their capitals. In partnership with robust peacekeeping, the concept of the protection of civilians (POC) has increasingly been discussed in peacekeeping circles.

Today, all large multidimensional UN peacekeeping mandates are embedded with a POC clause, which authorises missions to take action 'to protect civilians under the imminent threat of physical violence'.[6] UN peacekeeping is now firmly wedded to the concept of POC and, as a result, the credibility of the entire enterprise is arguably prefaced on the notion that missions should seek to actively protect civilians.

Yet, beyond these discussions of robustness and protection is the oft-neglected core of UN missions: the political process. This is the glue that binds the peace together, and without which positive peace[7] cannot be properly realised. The political process should drive every UN mission: 'peacekeeping is part of a political solution, not an alternative ... It must be engaged only as an accompaniment to an active political strategy.'[8] In spite of this, there exists little understanding as to what a political process or strategy actually entails, and how a peacekeeping mission should nurture such a process. The catchphrases of 'robust peacekeeping', 'the protection of civilians' and 'the political process' remain ambiguously defined. This book attempts to render clarity, not so much at the conceptual level, but at the level of application. It will achieve this by addressing a series of seemingly rudimentary questions: what is a political process? How do UN missions propagate or encourage its development, while balancing the demands of armed-group inclusion? What is robust peacekeeping? And how is the concept of POC best applied?

This *Adelphi* aims to provide a policy guide to UN missions and their engagement with armed groups. It contemplates the challenging nature of non-permissive UN mission environments, and offers a fresh way for the UN to think about how it undertakes missions in those difficult settings. This book is not intended to be overly critical, but to challenge conventional wisdom, which is healthy for any organisation. It advocates a rethink – a subtle reshaping of the way the UN goes about the business of peacekeeping and peacebuilding. A shift in thinking leads inevitably to the question of how the UN organises itself (both in New York and in the field) to understand and respond to the challenges and opportunities posed by armed groups. Any rethink must imbrue the UN with a more creative spirit in terms of its leadership, management, intelligence, tactics and strategy. This *Adelphi* suggests that the UN strive, in every mission environment, to understand the complexity of conflict and insecurity at a granular level, which does away with reductionist thinking, dominant peacebuilding narratives and well-recited talking points. Instead, UN missions should act in humility, with creativity and context sensitivity, and under more focused mandates.

Notes

1 David Kilcullen, *Out of the Mountains: The Coming Age of the Urban Guerilla* (New York: Oxford University Press, 2013), p. 34.

2 Stephen John Stedman, 'Spoiler Problems in Peace Processes', *International Security*, vol. 22, no. 2, Autumn 1997, p. 6.

3 *Ibid.*, p. 12.

4 Mats Berdal, 'Lessons Not Learned: The Use of Force in "Peace Operations' in the 1990s", *International Peacekeeping*, vol. 7, no. 4, November 2007, p. 58.

5 United Nations, *United Nations Peacekeeping Operations: Principles and Guidelines* (New York: United Nations), p. 35.

6 Victoria Holt and Glyn Taylor, *Protecting Civilians in the Context of UN Peacekeeping Operations: Successes, Setbacks and Remaining Challenges (Advance Copy)*, (New York: DPKO and OHCA, 2009), p. 285.

7 Positive peace is filled with positive content such as restoration of relationships, the creation of social systems that serve the needs of the whole population and the constructive resolution of conflict. See Claske Dijkema, 'Negative Verses Positive Peace', May 2007, http://www.irenees.net/en/fiches/notions/fiche-notions-186.html.

8 United Nations, *A New Partnership Agenda Charting a New Horizon for UN Peacekeeping* (New York: United Nations, 2009), p. iv.

CHAPTER ONE

Armed groups in modern warfare

Non-state armed groups are the main protagonists and antagonists in modern conflict. From the Democratic Republic of the Congo (DRC) to Central African Republic (CAR) to Darfur, South Sudan and Mali, armed groups are a fact of conflict. Understanding them, therefore, is key to bringing about peace and security. Yet, frequently, armed groups are overlooked, misunderstood or stigmatised. To provide a working definition, an armed group is a collection of individuals, bound by mutual influence and a common feeling of camaraderie, who employ the use of force to achieve a set of political, social, economic or ideological goals but are not members of the regular armed forces or security services. This chapter examines why armed groups mobilise, why individuals choose to join them and how they sustain their capacity to fight.

Roots of conflict

Armed groups do not emerge from a social or political vacuum. Rather, they emerge in response to a particular set of conditions – a grievance, insecurity, an interest (vested or communal) or an opportunity. In this respect, armed groups are tied to the root causes of conflict: ethnic tension and predation; captured states; horizontal inequalities; self-serving leadership; regional distortions; land-use issues; environmental consequences of climate change; as well as a host of historical, social and political injustices.

Governance and political economy

The collapse of political order is often a result of structural inequalities embedded in the political economy of the state. In many conflict-afflicted states, winner-takes-all politics are practised, which creates conflict. In simple terms, government is the prize that allows access to economic resources. Quite often, such an exclusive system is buttressed by clientism (or patronage politics), whereby goods and services are exchanged for political support. Ethnic exclusivity is also often the hallmark of such systems: presidents favouring their own ethnic group to the exclusion of others – in multi-ethnic states. Prior to the civil war in Sierra Leone, only one party ruled the country: the All People's Congress (APC) and its leaders Sitka Stevens and Joseph Said Momoh. These leaders instituted an oppressive state apparatus, which favoured the cronies of the APC and oppressed the voices of opposition and dissent. Behind the façade of the APC's oppressive apparatus, a shadow state resided. The APC, under Stevens and to a lesser extent Momoh, used the proceeds of diamond mining and asset stripping to maintain the patronage of important chieftains, power brokers and the military.

Political and economic marginalisation can also manifest in core–periphery terms: the core is the centre of political and economic life (the capital) and the periphery is usually an outlying region. If conditions are ripe, underdevelopment coupled with marginalisation can cause those in the periphery to rebel against the central government. *The Black Book: the Imbalance of Power and Wealth in Sudan* argued that the political elite of the North (the riverine Arab clans of the Shaigiya, Jaaliyeen and the Danagla) held a monopoly on power, which had led to the marginalisation and neglect of the outlying regions. The distribution of the book in the early 2000s was a clarion call for the rebel groups in Darfur, which immediately began to step up their resistance to the centre in Khartoum. The argument is that those excluded from the system are likely to rebel against the powers that be, while those in power are likely to develop mechanisms to eliminate rivals, and strengthen their grip by delimiting the political space. Inequality does not itself create the conditions for conflict. Rather, the conflict-creating device is 'inequality without opportunity – permanent exclusion, marginalization without hope of improving one's circum-stances – [this] can create lethal ... resentments, when people who realise they can never join the party decide to burn the house instead.'[1] Armed groups rise on the back of these resent-ments.

Resources

Land is a particularly pernicious issue, an economic resource which supports agricultural livelihoods, but also a signifi-cant cultural marker of belonging. In El Salvador, the unequal distribution of land was one of the central grievances of the rural-based rebel movement – the Farabundo Martí National Liberation Front (FMLN). Land ownership was concentrated in the hands of the nation's landed elite, most of whom grew coffee, while the campesinos, the rural peasantry, eked out an existence through subsistence farming. Prior to the civil war '40% of families were landless and less than 2% of families held more than 10 hectares'.[2]

Land and water are contested resources in Central Africa and the Sahel. In these regions conflicts between nomadic pastoralists and sedentary farmers have occurred due to shifting patterns of land use. As 'pastoral ecosystems transcend borders and transhumance',[3] even subtle shifts in the environment can result in 'new settlement fronts', that in turn create friction between the two communities.[4] In the early 2000s, a persistent drought in Darfur contributed to a conflict between nomadic Arab tribes and the sedentary farmers of the Zur and other groups. Rainfall in sub-Saharan Africa may decrease by 30% by the 2080s, while the Sahara desert continues to expand; it is reasonable to expect these developments to drive conflicts in the future. After all, shifts in climate have a marked effect on human settlement, land-use patterns and, by extension, on the capacity of governance structures.

Regional context

Regional context must also be considered in assessing the drivers of conflict: the 'bad neighbourhood' effect, for example, as well as overall regional power dynamics. Conflict rarely conforms to the boundaries of the state; in fact, many conflicts transcend borders and come to resemble vast regional complexes bound together by shared human terrain and economies. In most instances, the so-called regionalisation of conflict is not merely a case of spillover, but of conflict made by regional dynamics. In certain regions of Africa, for example, governments have been accused of supporting insurgencies in their neighbouring countries through the direct support of rebel groups. Certain regions are mired in a criss-cross of proxy campaigns. In the early 2000s, Chad entered into a 'state of belligerence' with the Government of Sudan (GoS). In this case, the GoS supported Chadian rebels against the Idriss Déby regime, while the Chadian government supported the Darfuri rebel group the Justice and Equality Movement (JEM). In the Horn of Africa, long-running rivalry between Eritrea and

Ethiopia has played out as a proxy campaign in neighbouring Somalia, with Ethiopia supporting the Federal Government of Somalia against an Al-Shabaab supported Eritrea. In the DRC, a succession of armed groups – the Rally for Congolese Democracy (RCD)-Goma, the National Congress for the Defence of the People (CNDP) and the March 23 Movement (M23) – were supported by the Rwandan government, as part of a proxy campaign designed to secure Rwandan interests in the country.

Catalysts

Lastly, depending on the prevalence of underlying volatilities, spontaneous or planned demonstrations, violent government crackdowns, or mismanaged, stolen or fraudulent elections all can have a catalytic effect. Tit-for-tat violence can rapidly escalate into conflict and lead to the creation of a plethora of new groups, as individuals respond to insecurity by mobilising to protect their communities. During the revolutions in Tunisia, Egypt, Libya and Syria, a cycle of protests and violent regime repression was witnessed. In certain key cases, regime security forces targeted activists at funerals. These would later prove to be poignant catalysts for further protests, and in turn further regime repression. The regimes of Zine El Abidine Ben Ali, Hosni Mubarak, Muammar Gadhafi and Bashar al-Assad, therefore, inadvertently created 'self-replenishing cycle[s] of violence'.[5]

The drivers of intra-state conflict are multiple, layered and difficult, if not impossible, to completely comprehend. Intra-state conflict is a messy, opaque and ever-evolving mosaic.

Motivation (purpose and identities)

It is often difficult to know what motivates an armed group, as the leadership might itself have conflicting ideas about what

the group actually stands for. There are many labels assigned
to armed groups, with differing responses deemed appropriate for dealing with them. The application of labels has led
to prejudiced responses to individual armed groups. Across
a range of contexts, particular observable commonalities do
exist between groups, which makes a broad categorisation or
typology somewhat viable. Clearly, certain groups inhabit a
particular identity to serve their particular political or economic
ends. A glossary of identities appears in the Appendix.

Crucially, armed groups do not necessarily ascribe to a
single unified identity but rather to multiple identities, as
conflict is ever evolving and motives mixed. As Jason Stearns
has rightly suggested, armed groups 'tend to develop their
own dynamics and interests, becoming dislocated from the
forces that initially gave birth to them'.[6] Groups such as Raia
Mutomboki or the Mai-Mai groups of Eastern Congo may have
started out as self-defence groups, but their identity quickly
morphed. Other groups are driven by enterprise. As a conflict
develops, so do the opportunities for rent-seeking behaviour.
The collapse of the formal economy and the growth of an illicit
economy creates opportunities for conflict entrepreneurs. The
Revolutionary United Front (RUF), which operated in Sierra
Leone and Liberia during the Sierra Leonean civil war (1991–
2002), is another example. The RUF began as a loose collection
of individuals who had trained in Benghazi, Libya in the late
1980s. The group espoused a set of revolutionary objectives that
it sought to pursue in alliance with Charles Taylor's National
Patriotic Front of Liberia (NPFL). Despite its revolutionary
pronouncements ('basic rights for all'), the group comprised
the njiahungbia ngonga – that is, 'riff raff, lumpen and unruly
youth',[7] who engaged in banditry and committed mass atrocities against the rural peasantry, thereby eroding their potential
base of popular support.[8] This behaviour of the RUF revealed

the true nature of the group. Essentially, the RUF practised the politics of the gun, and was therefore less a revolutionary group and more a warlord army or group of bandits, intent on exploiting mineral wealth.

Recruitment

The rationales for joining, and then continuing to fight in, a group are diverse, and each fighter will likely have a different story to tell. Nevertheless, armed groups around the world employ a small range of tried-and-tested recruiting strategies, many of which seek to gain emotional or rational hold over would-be volunteer recruits. In the Eastern DRC, groups such as the M23 or the Allied Democratic Forces-Nalu (ADF-Nalu) lure potential recruits with the promise of employment and/or education. Other M23 recruits were motivated by the promise of material gain. These fighters were never paid during their service; instead, they worked on the basis of a promised future pay-off: 'we were sustained on hope that one day they would pay us.'[9]

Forcible recruitment, particularly of children, attracts much attention. Groups that employ this method usually attempt to break down a recruit psychologically, and build them up again in the image of a merciless fighter. In some cases, children are forced to commit atrocities against their own communities, even killing their own families, so as to sever familial and communal bonds. These abducted children have no home to then go back to and few options apart from embracing the group, its leaders and its ideology. In a way, the group becomes their de facto family.

Indoctrination is a powerful instrument used to maintain group cohesion and guard against desertion. It is common, in military organisations, for a process of group socialisation to take hold, which instils an *esprit de corps*. This is important for commanders faced with little prospect of victory, because as the war drags on, soldiers come to fight for their comrades, rather than an illusory cause. Socialisation is the most effective method for maintaining membership, as opposed to coercion or fear, which work against group cohesion and morale. The ADF-Nalu is one such group governed by fear, with its leaders brutally killing any soldier 'caught trying to escape by beheading or ... crucifixion'.[10]

Besides indoctrination and coercion, groups can use status (material wealth) to continually motivate fighters. The Lord's Resistance Army (LRA), for instance, has instituted a system to regulate morale and drive battlefield performance. The system is based on a division between officers and fighters. While officers of the LRA are awarded perks (wives, transistor radios and protection), the soldiers are exposed to the greatest danger (at the rear or front of the line). In order to gain a promotion, fighters must prove themselves in combat – displaying bravery is rewarded. The upward mobility of the LRA lies in contrast to the Democratic Forces for the Liberation of Rwanda (FDLR), who operate on the basis of a 'divide between Rwandan commanders who own fields and the rest of the troops who are told to loot to survive'.[11] It is no surprise that under these conditions morale among FDLR fighters has not been particularly strong, with a high rate of surrender.

Popular support

Armed groups can enjoy widespread popular support, either across society, or among a particular demographic or interest group. Insurgency depends on popular support:

> The guerrilla band ... draws its great force from the mass of the people themselves ... Guerrilla warfare is used by the side which is supported by a majority but

which possesses a much smaller number of arms for use in defence against oppression.[12]

The FMLN in El Salvador, too, clearly represented a significant portion of Salvadoran society (trade unionists, intellectuals, rural peasantry and the Catholic church) – a portion which had been excluded from the political process by the party of government, ARENA, backed by an agrarian oligarchy.

There are groups that operate devoid of popular support; they will mostly act as fringe groups pursuing limited goals – usually profit.

The theory of competitive control provides a more sophisticated analysis of the complex interaction between populations and armed groups. According to this theory, for armed groups to endure they must master the arts of coercion, administration and persuasion. Populations crave security – a predictable order in which they can live out their lives. If armed groups recognise this fact, they can seek to build, own and operate a rules-based system in order to control a particular population. The foundation of this system is coercion: the ability of the group to enforce its order through use of punitive violence, as well as to protect the system from competitors, and punish defectors. An armed group becomes truly dominant in an area only when the population adheres to its rule set. Groups which rely on, and govern solely through, fear and coercion are, on the other hand, relatively brittle. A more mature and resilient group will wield the instruments of administration and persuasion to greater effect – locking a community into a set of positive incentive structures.

Groups can use persuasion to draw populations into supporting their order. Persuasion in this sense is exercised through propaganda, social and political ideology, and social pressure, reinforced by an overriding atmosphere of insecurity. Once a level of security is created in a particular area, an armed group can establish an administration to provide material benefit to the rules-following population. The provision of informal justice, dispute resolution and mediation (particularly in regard to property rights), policing, infrastructure and economic institutions are the hallmark administrative functions of highly developed non-state armed groups. In certain communities, the system described is so sophisticated that the group, as a dispensary of public goods, resembles something akin to de facto government. The Lebanese Shia political militia Hizbullah is arguably the greatest exponent of sophisticated competitive control. Hizbullah has mastered the art of administration and persuasion, through the expert management of its social-development programme: 'Hezbollah [does] everything that a government should do, from collecting the garbage to running hospitals and repairing schools.'[13] The group uses an array of front-line agencies to deliver an impressive range of social services including infrastructure reconstruction, health, education and media. At the other end of the spectrum are groups that seem 'uninterested in winning converts, content instead to steal other people's children, stick Kalashnikovs or axes in their hands, and make them do the killing'.[14] Clearly, there are a whole host of groups that show no inclination towards establishing a base of popular support or even controlling a population.

Logistics

Questions of logistics have long concerned military strategists, commanders and national leaders – from Sun Tzu to the present. The limitations of military supply chains are all too evident. Even the sophisticated supply routes of the International Security Assistance Force (ISAF) in Afghanistan, for example, have been disrupted by Taliban attacks. Non-state armed groups, however, face a different set of logistical problems, which relate to the covert sourcing of weapons and materiel. In order to fight, armed groups, like militaries, must possess weapons, ammunition and basic supplies (food and medicine). An armed group seeking improved mobility, firepower and communications might also need to invest in, or acquire more, sophisticated military hardware. Armed groups have a number of options when it comes to sourcing weapons and materiel.

They can steal weapons, materiel and supplies from the caches or depots of the government or rival groups. For example, in August 2013, Syrian rebels seized a weapons depot north of Damascus. By doing so, they acquired Russian-made 9M113 *Konkurs* and *Grad* missiles, as well as French-made MILIAN anti-tank guided missiles. In the DRC, the ADF-Nalu attacked the town of Kamango in July 2013 with the express purpose of 'stockpiling drugs and medical equipment'.[15]

It might, however, be easier or more expeditious for armed groups to simply make weapons and military hardware themselves. In real terms armed groups, and particularly loosely organised militias, might not have any apparent alternatives. The anti-Balaka in CAR took up arms using improvised means – home-made machetes and guns. Increasingly, armed groups are repurposing household and off-the-shelf products. In Syria, rebels have constructed home-made rocket launchers and mortars. Even more sophisticated, an armoured vehicle was built with a remotely operated machine gun activated using a PlayStation controller. More than ever before, advances in technology and increasing Internet connectivity allow armed groups to build strong global cyberspace networks in order to secure weapons, receive training and get crowd-sourced funding for their activities.

Weapons can also be supplied to armed groups by a foreign patron. Groups can either be wholly owned subsidiaries of foreign patrons (operating on behalf of an outside power) or they can rely on limited, conditional or occasional support from outside backers. According to the reports of the Panel of Experts on the DRC, M23 received deliveries of weapons and ammunition via the Kabuhanga-Kabuye crossing with Rwanda. Credible sources attested to Rwanda's complicity with the M23, stating that, 'ammunition usually came at night in trucks, and included rifle and machine gun ammunition, 12.7 mm rounds, anti-tank rounds and rocket-propelled grenades'.[16] Foreign backers are not always foreign governments. Quite often funding for armed groups is derived from expansive global networks; ghost charities, for example, have been known to channel funds to various groups, as is particularly the case with the Taliban. It is also not uncommon for armed groups to receive funding through remittances sent from diaspora communities. Al-Shabaab in Somalia, for instance, uses the *hawala* system.

Weapons and materiel can also be bought by armed groups – arguably the most common method by which weapons are acquired. In order to purchase weaponry, a group must have adequate and reliable funding arrangements. Depending on its level of problem-solving nous, a group may levy a criminal rent, or simply loot to extract the necessary funds and resources. If armed groups utilise the instrument of administration, they can impose household, transport and business taxes to fund their activities, and in some cases reinvest in community infrastructure. For example, in the areas under its control, the M23 became proficient in the use of roadblocks to extort money from drivers on roads across the region. The group even imposed a de facto customs duty on vehicles crossing the Ugandan frontier at Bungana. However, as the group began to 'lose strength', its fighters resorted to the looting of 'money and goods from local populations'.[17]

Many groups operating in countries, regions or enclaves rich in natural resources tend to finance their activities through the exploitation of those resources – timber, oil, gold, coltan, cassiterite, rough diamonds, ivory and charcoal. Three principal exponents of this practice are the National Union for the Total Independence of Angola (UNITA), RUF in Sierra Leone and the Islamic State of Iraq and al-Sham (ISIS) in Western Iraq and Eastern Syria. Groups exploiting natural resources in such a fashion might either seek to directly control a resource (such as a mine or alluvial diamond water course), tax the extracted resource, or stage one-off attacks on resource-rich areas. The very well-financed ISIS can afford to pay its fighters US$400 a month due, in large part, to its control of oilfields, as well as taxation, kidnapping and ransom.[18] In the DRC, Mai-Mai Morgan, a group operating in the Haut Uélé and Ituri, has been known to poach elephants, but in late 2013 turned to raiding gold mines.

Using the funds accrued through the various methods described above, armed groups can buy weapons (or trade minerals). At the conclusion of the Cold War, a huge arms market opened across Eastern Europe. The opportunities afforded by this opening were exploited by a generation of gunrunners, the most notorious being Viktor Bout and Leonid Minin. Both men forged the end-user certificates of weapons shipments in order to circumvent arms controls. Even with the new Arms Trade Treaty (ATT) in place, the black market still remains the easiest way for armed groups to acquire high-rate weaponry at a reasonable price.[19]

Command and Control (C2)

How do armed groups maintain control of their fighting force? Why do armed groups enter into alliances? Certain armed groups might be highly structured organisations with a military chain of command, while others might resemble a disorganised mob or swarm. Each group organises itself differently, and employs tactics derived from their different circumstances.

In order to be successful in pursuing its goals, 'an armed group must have a leadership cadre with the ability to direct its members'.[20] This relies in part on 'some level of hierarchical organisation and discipline'.[21] Organic, networked command structures allow sub-unit or cell commanders a high degree of flexibility, as well as independence to conduct operations and designate certain targets in accordance with an overarching strategy defined by high command. On the other hand, a more linear hierarchical structure requires a system of discipline akin to that involved in professional soldiering. Organisational structure varies greatly from group to group, and is usually reflective of the threat environment in which a group operates, as well as its political, social and cultural setting, the imperatives of resourcing and the dominant thinking of the group's leadership cadre. An armed group's structure, modus operandi and area of operations also depend on the motivations of the group. While a civil-defence militia group which aims to protect its kin will usually allow its fighters to live amongst the population, an insurgent group, on the other hand, might establish a base of operations in a more remote area (forest or mountainous, for example).

The FDLR has a command structure reminiscent of a national army, with a chief of staff and sector and sub-sector commanders. The group also employs an elite group composed of experienced soldiers called the Commando de recherché et d'action en profondeur, which is deployed in areas of strategic importance in North and South Kivu. In addition to these specialised units, the FDLR created the Postes d'intervention populaire (PIP) to protect Rwandan Hutu refugee populations in the region. The most sophisticated armed groups will fundamentally alter their organisation, tactics and even their entire raison d'être when under threat – to ensure the group's survival. The FDLR, for instance, disperses 'and scatter[s] into the forest when attacked. In addition, FDLR combatants live with their women and children; military operations risk causing collateral damage...[one] source identified about 22 small FDLR locations (11 in South Kivu and 11 in North Kivu), in which combatants often stay with their families.'[22] Likewise, and perhaps even more so, the LRA, when attacked by the Uganda People's Defence Force, atomised and now operates in separate groups across a large swath of territory. The atomisation of the group fundamentally reshaped the organisation and its modus operandi; where once the LRA was a rebellion, today it has been 'reduced to a marauding outfit'.[23]

The leadership cadre is a collection of individuals, each with their own history, experience, skills, ambitions, motives and gripes. The interactions that take place between these individuals and constitute the group's internal dynamics or politics are important to consider. Divergent opinions expressed regarding strategy, tactics, a political path or the details of a peace agreement can cause in-group turmoil, which can lead to fractionalisation and even a splintering of the group. Splintering, and conversely alliance-building, is a common theme of multi-party civil war; there is a 'tendency for intergroup alliances in multiparty conflict to shift constantly, and for groups themselves to be perpetually at risk of internal splits and takeovers'.[24] The rationale behind alliance-making and splintering is relative power considerations:

> Warring groups in multiparty civil wars ... dwell in an anarchic environment where they seek to not only survive, but also to profit. As a result, each group seeks to form wartime intergroup alliances that constitute

minimum winning coalitions: alliances with enough aggregate power to win the conflict.[25]

Divergences can also occur when a group structurally separates its military and political functions. The Irish Republican Army (IRA) and Sinn Féin are one such example. It is common for many groups or group members to also actively collaborate with government officials through accommodation, cooperation or appropriation. As previously mentioned, certain groups become wholly owned subsidiaries of governments, or the party of government, to intimidate voters, rally support or respond to protests by opposition groups.

The training afforded to fighters is also important to consider, as the duration and quality of training undoubtedly improves a group's battlefield performance. Even simple close-order drills can instil military discipline, build unit cohesion and provide the basis for military action and mobility. While a group like the LRA offers no more than on-the-job training, the ADF-Nalu undertakes four-month-long boot camps, and even conducts covert-operations training. The group's ambush training has been described as 'noteworthy for its disciplined and professional directives'.[26]

Tactics employed by groups vary widely (defensive, offensive, small-unit and covert), depending on a fighter's training and a commander's competence. Under the command of former professional soldiers, armed groups will perform relatively conventionally or might adopt an asymmetric posture – hit-and-run attacks, ambushes and use of improvised explosive devices, for example. It is not uncommon for a group to devise a set of tried-and-tested tactics, and apply them as a matter of routine. The Taliban is one group that routinely applies highly effective ambush tactics. Even seemingly chaotic, disorganised tactical manoeuvres may belie a more organised mindset.

The rule-based self-synchronising swarm tactics employed by Somali militias are a case in point. Although seemingly chaotic, swarm tactics operate under a simple set of rules, which, if followed by each individual fighter, places them in a position of semi-autonomy, and gives them unparalleled flexibility and mobility. The beauty of the system is such that 'the swarm's command system is distributed, rule-based, emergent, and thus embedded in the system itself, not tied to any one person, vehicle or physical location'.[27]

In order to direct action or enact strategy, commanders must be able to communicate orders to their troops. Depending on the circumstances, this can be relatively easy or incredibly difficult. Commanders who fight alongside their troops can simply relay instructions up the line or via two-way radio. Those commanders not on the battlefield, however, have a more difficult task; they must direct action from afar, communicating via voice calls (satellite and cellular), text messages, email, Skype, Twitter, Facebook, geocaching, dead-letter drops and other covert techniques.

FDLR commanders communicate with geographically disparate units through the use of satellite phone. Joseph Kony also used satellite phones, but ceased the practice due to his fear that the LRA task force would use signal triangulation to locate the position of his forces. With the ever-widening cellular-phone coverage offered by telecommunications companies across the world, groups can now easily access standard GSM coverage for communications purposes. For instance, al-Qaeda in the Islamic Maghreb (AQIM), when operating in Mali, was known to exploit the Algerian cellular network.[28] While new technologies are enabling better communication, some groups continue to use supposedly outmoded forms of communication (including two-way radios, coded notebooks and runners) out of fear of interception. The LRA, for example, has in recent years returned to the method of running messages to its independent battle-groups.

It is clear that the motivations, organisation and operations of armed groups are complex; they adapt constantly to the environment in which they develop. Differing identities, levels of popular support and logistics, for example, all influence how groups fight. There are myriad challenges, therefore, that UN missions face in seeking to deal with armed groups in order to restore peace and stability.

Notes

1 David Kilcullen, *Out of the Mountains: The Coming Age of the Urban Guerilla* (New York: Oxford University Press, 2013), pp. 246–7.

2 USAID, *El Salvador Property Rights and Resource Governance Profile* (Washington DC: USAID, 2011), p. 3.

3 See 'The Security Challenges of Pastoralism in Central Africa' International Crisis Group, 1 April 2014, http://www.crisisgroup. org/en/publication-type/media-releases/2014/africa/the-security-challenges-of-pastorialism-in-central-africa.aspx.

4 *Ibid.*

5 David Kilcullen, *Out of the Mountains: The Coming Age of the Urban Guerilla* (New York: Oxford University Press, 2013), p. 184.

6 Jason Stearns et al., *Raia Mutomkoki: The Flawed Peace Process in the DRC and the Birth of an Armed Franchise* (London and Nairobi: Rift Valley Institute, 2013), p. 39.

7 Ibrahim Abdullah, 'Bush Path to Destruction: the Origin and Character of the Revolutionary United Front/Sierra Leone', *Journal of Modern Africa Studies*, vol. 36, no. 2, June 1998, p. 224.

8 *Ibid.*

9 Group of Experts on Democratic Republic of the Congo, *Final Report of the Group of Experts on the Democratic Republic of the Congo* (New York: United Nations, 2014), p. 11.

10 *Ibid.*, p. 19.

11 *Ibid.*

12 Ernesto Guevara, *Guerrilla Warfare* (Wilmington, DE: Scholarly Resources Inc., 1997), p. 52.

13 See Henry Schuster, 'Hezbollah's Secret Weapon', CNN, 26 July 2006, http://edition.cnn.com/2006/ WORLD/meast/07/24/schuster. hezbollah/index.html.

14 See Jeffrey Gettleman, 'Africa's Forever Wars: Why the Continent's Conflicts Never End', *Foreign Policy*, 22 February 2010, http://www. foreignpolicy.com/articles/2010/02/ 22/africas_forever_wars.

15 Group of Experts on Democratic Republic of the Congo, *Final Report of the Group of Experts on the*

Democratic Republic of the Congo, p. 20.

16 *Ibid.,* p. 9.

17 *Ibid.*

18 'The Economist Explains Where Islamic State Gets Its Money', *The Economist*, 4 January 2015, http://www.economist.com/blogs/economist-explains/2015/01/economist-explains?fsrc=scn/tw/te/bl/ee/whereislamicstategetsitsmoney.

19 In some markets that are awash with weapons, an AK-47 assault rifle can retail for as little as US$90.

20 Alex Vinci, 'The "Problems of Mobilization" and the Analysis of Armed Groups', *Parameters*, vol. 36, no. 1, Spring 2006, p. 56.

21 *Ibid,* pp. 56–7.

22 Group of Experts on Democratic Republic of the Congo, *Final Report of the Group of Experts on the Democratic Republic of the Congo*, p. 25.

23 *Ibid.*

24 Fotini Christia, *Alliance Formation in Civil Wars* (New York: Cambridge University Press, 2012).

25 *Ibid.*

26 Group of Experts on Democratic Republic of the Congo, *Final Report of the Group of Experts on the Democratic Republic of the Congo*, p. 20.

27 David Kilcullen, *Out of the Mountains*, p. 85.

28 Robert Fowler, *A Season in Hell: My 130 Days in the Sahara with al Qaeda* (Toronto: Harper Collins, 2011)

CHAPTER TWO

Forming a response: UN missions

In late 1956, Egypt nationalised the Suez Canal Company, provoking a military response by France, the United Kingdom and Israel. The Israelis quickly captured territory on the Sinai Peninsula, while British and French forces undertook airborne operations against Port Said and Alexandria. Despite these swift victories, international pressure began to mount on the three powers. With the United Nations Security Council deadlocked, following UK and French vetoes, the matter of Suez was taken to the General Assembly under the 'Uniting for Peace' resolution. During an emergency session, Canadian Secretary of State for External Affairs Lester B. Pearson recognised that a ceasefire and withdrawal would not be sufficient, and proposed the establishment of an international force to 'police' the ceasefire between Israeli, French and British forces on one side, and the Egyptians on the other.

The General Assembly endorsed Pearson's idea,[1] and the then-secretary-general Dag Hammarskjöld hastily worked to develop a guiding doctrine for the new interpositional force, which was to be known as the United Nations Emergency Force (UNEF I). Hammarskjöld's guiding principles for UNEF

– the consent of the parties, impartiality and the non-*use of force* except in self-defence – would come to define and guide peacekeeping throughout the Cold War era and beyond. The UN had crafted, albeit through improvisation, a new conflict-management instrument for itself – peacekeeping.

Hammarskjöld's guiding principles for UNEF soon became the bedrock upon which all UN missions would rest. Essentially, these principles accepted that the UN could 'cajole, argue, bluster ... but [it could not] compel'.[2] A UN mission, it was argued, could only operate with the consent of the parties to the conflict. Whilst positioned between consenting parties, UN missions would act as tripwires, and would not seek to favour one party over the other or impose a Security Council-mandated settlement. Hammarskjöld remarked that 'it follows for the rule that the UN units must not become parties to internal conflicts, that they cannot be used to enforce or to influence the political balance decisive to such a solution.'[3] Given that they would operate impartially and with the consent of the parties involved, peacekeepers would only need to be lightly armed – to protect themselves, and do no more. According to Hammarskjöld the principle of the non-use of force prohibited military initiative: an 'operation may never take the initiative in the use of armed force, but [is] entitled to respond with force to an attack with arms ... the basic element involved is clearly the prohibition against any initiative in the use of armed force.'[4]

Most peacekeeping operations conducted during the Cold War era subscribed to these principles, and practised the traditional mode of peacekeeping; the UN would act as an inter-positional force between two opposing armies, after a ceasefire agreement was signed. There were, however, exceptions, the most contentious and radical of which was the deployment of peacekeepers to the Democratic Republic of the Congo (DRC) in 1960, during a period of turmoil following the country's independence from Belgium. A cascading set of crises began first with the mutiny of the Congolese military, then the deployment of Belgian forces without the consent of the Congolese government, before culminating in an attempted secession of the provinces of Katanga and South Kasai. The Congolese prime minister, Patrice Lumumba, and president Joseph Kasavubu subsequently called on the UN for assistance.

Hammarskjöld and the Security Council responded by establishing the United Nations Operation in the Congo (ONUC) to oversee the withdrawal of Belgian forces and assist the Congolese authorities in restoring order. However, in September 1960, the DRC was plunged into a constitutional crisis, following Lumumba's removal from office after he had requested Soviet military assistance to suppress the secessionist rebellions. A CIA-backed coup, staged by Colonel Joseph Mobutu, was successful in establishing a pro-Western regime in Léopoldville. ONUC soon became embroiled in questions concerning the use of force. The Security Council authorised the use of force 'to prevent the occurrence of civil war in the Congo',[5] but ambiguities remained regarding which faction ONUC would target and under what circumstances. Using Resolutions 161 and 169 as their mandate, UN forces launched a series of operations (*Rumpunch*, *Morthor*, *Unokat* and *Grand Slam*) against the Katangese separatists and their foreign supporters. Although many of these operations were poorly conducted and politically tenuous, the UN was eventually able to restore Katanga to the Congo, in what some have described as a 'pyrrhic victory at best'.[6] The narrative of ONUC provided a remarkable glimpse into the future of peacekeeping: one characterised as intra-state and complex. Like ONUC, multidimensional peacekeeping in the future would also be wrought by questions of force and intrusiveness.

ONUC was the first of what were later termed multidimensional peacekeeping missions. This type of mission defined the immediate post-Cold War era of peacekeeping, as the Security Council attempted to address the lingering proxy wars of the 1990s. Multidimensional missions were woven into the fabric of respective peace processes, aiming to boost confidence building among civil-war parties. Today, these missions are 'composed of a range of components including military, civilian police, political, civil affairs, rule of law, human rights, humanitarian, reconstruction, public information and gender'.[7] They occur within the liberal-peace paradigm, by conducting de facto state-building and assisting fledgling governments to consolidate authority and rule of law within a democratic framework.

The end of the Cold War created a space in which many long-running civil wars could be peacefully resolved. In Namibia, Mozambique, El Salvador and Cambodia, UN missions were deployed to oversee the implementation of peace agreements within each country that had been negotiated between incumbent governments and opposing armed rebel groups. The missions themselves were authorised under Chapter VI of the Charter, which prohibited them from launching offensive operations against spoilers. Under these circumstances, UN missions essentially acted as insurance policies, underwriting their respective peace agreements through constant mediation and confidence-building measures.

United Nations Transition Assistance Group (UNTAG) in Namibia, United Nations Operation in Mozambique (ONUMOZ), United Nations Observer Mission in El Salvador (ONUSAL), and United Nations Transitional Administration in Cambodia (UNTAC) were each troubled by instances of intransigence. In Namibia, a South West Africa People's Organization (SWAPO) incursion from neighbouring Angola, on day one of the peace, almost resulted in the unravelling of the New York Accords. In El Salvador, the discovery of FMLN weapons caches, coupled with persistent government obstructionism (in relation to the land-transfer programme, demobilisation of the National Police and truth and reconciliation commission) severely challenged the implementation of the Chapultepec Peace Accords. In Mozambique, initial deployment of UN peacekeepers occurred amidst an atmosphere of distrust between Mozambican National Resistance (RENAMO) and the government, following the signing of the Rome Peace Agreement. In Cambodia, the Khmer Rouge refused to disarm (in accordance with their obligations), and later withdrew completely from the Paris Peace Accords.[8]

In 1992, amidst this unprecedented build-up in peacekeeping operations, the then-secretary-general Boutros Boutros-Ghali delivered a report, entitled *An Agenda for Peace*, seeking to clarify definitions of key terms. These were: preventive diplomacy; peacemaking; peacekeeping; and a new concept termed 'post-conflict peacebuilding'. Peace-enforcement units were also suggested as an option, allowing the Security Council to 'respond to outright aggression, imminent or actual'.[9] Two of the UN's toughest tests followed in Yugoslavia and Somalia, after which the spirit of activism captured in the *Agenda for Peace* was replaced by retrenchment.

Yugoslavia: UNPROFOR

As Yugoslavia began to disintegrate, conflicts between the secessionist republics and the Yugoslav government in Belgrade (essentially a Serbian core) consumed the Balkans. The most intense fighting happened between Serbs and Croats in Croatia, and Serbs, Croats and Bosniaks in Bosnia-Herzegovina. In both Croatia and Bosnia, the conflict comprised a patchwork of regular, irregular and criminal groups. Each national faction maintained a national defence establishment, supported by a plethora of paramilitary groups. The Serbs commanded the remnants of the Yugoslav People's Army (JNA), and later formed the Army of Republican Ruska (VRS) reinforced by the Serb White Eagles, Arkan's Tigers, and the Serbian Volunteer Guard, among others. In Bosnia, the Bosniaks founded the Army of the Republic of Bosnia and Herzegovina (ARBiH), supported by the Territorial Defence Force of the Republic of Bosnia and Herzegovina (TORBIH), the Patriotic League (PL), Zelene Beretke (Green Berets) and Crni Labudovi (Black Swans). The Croats, in both Croatia and Bosnia, held to their national defence force, the Croatian Defence Council (HVO), and a host of paramilitary groups including the Croatian Defence Forces (Hrvatske Obrambene Snage).

It was amidst these armed groups that the United Nations Protection Force (UNPROFOR) was established to monitor ceasefires, first in Croatia, then in Bosnia. The Security Council also charged UNPROFOR with the task of verifying the integrity of several UN Protection Areas (UNPAs) in Serbian-populated regions of Croatia. As the conflict spread into Bosnia, following the independence referendum, ethnic cleansing became a routine practice. By late 1992, the situation in Bosnia was characterised by widespread ethnic cleansing and mass atrocity crimes. With the shift in the conflict came a corresponding shift in UNPROFOR's mandate, which was expanded to securing delivery of humanitarian aid. Without a ceasefire to monitor, UNPROFOR was forced to conduct its humanitarian-convoy activities on the basis of consent. Under these conditions, aid delivery quickly became a game of obstructionism and taxation for the warlords.

In the midst of the conflict, Bosniak, Croat and the Serb regular and paramilitary forces fought to control and maintain territory. Another shift in policy and mandate occurred in the spring of 1993, when the Security Council decided to deploy an extra 7,600 troops (with close-air support provided by NATO) to deter armed attacks against six designated safe areas, which had been besieged by Bosnian Serb forces: Srebrenica, Sarajevo, Zepa, Gorazde, Tuzla and Bihac.[10] The resolutions establishing these six safe areas were loosely worded, and did not actually specifically reference the protection of civilians. Rather, they demanded that Bosnian Serb military and paramilitary units cease attacks there and withdraw to 'a distance wherefrom they [Serb forces]' would cease to 'constitute a menace' to the security of the townships and 'that of their inhabitants'.[11]

The secretary-general advised the council that the deployment of the extra 7,600 troops was considered 'light', and would only ensure protection of the safe zones through deterrence, rather than physical presence. Throughout 1994, Bosnian Serb forces became wise to the weaknesses of the safe areas and began systematically testing their defences. In July 1995, units of the VRS (under the command of Ratko Mladic) surrounded Srebrenica. A 400-strong battalion of Dutch peacekeepers was garrisoned in the township under the auspices of the Resolution 819 safe-area plan. The Dutch battalion was severely outnumbered, and although the peacekeepers fired warning shots and let off flares in an attempt to dissuade the advance of Bosnian Serb forces, the peacekeepers never directly engaged any Bosnian Serb units. On 10 July, Bosnian Serb forces captured the town, and later massacred 7,000 Bosniaks, mostly men and boys.

In reaction to the takeover of the safe areas (Zepa was also overrun), the UK, France and the Netherlands committed troops to a new Rapid Reaction Force (RRF) with more robust rules of engagement. The UN decided to pursue peace enforcement and in August 1995, NATO, in coordination with the RRF, launched offensive operations against the VRS. From Mount Igman, the RRF began to shell VRS artillery positions around

Sarajevo – an action that effectively ended the siege of the city. Additionally, *Operation Storm* shifted the battlelines in favour of the Croats. In 1995, the Dayton and Erdut Peace Agreements finally brought an end to the conflicts in both Bosnia and Croatia.

Somalia

As UNPROFOR became mired in its own struggles, another set of UN missions deployed to Somalia were beset by similar problems. The situation in Somalia began with the overthrow of the country's long-time military ruler Syed Bare in 1991. Bare was ousted by a coalition of militias, which included the Somali National Movement (SNM), the Somali National Alliance (SNA), the United Somali Congress (USC) and the Somali Salvation Democratic Front (SSDF). The coalition was short-lived and a civil war began between the various rebels; Ali Mahdi Muhammad (interim president) led the USC/SSDF, while Mohamed Farah Aidid led the USC/SNA. The state subsequently collapsed, creating anarchy, made worse by a drought-induced famine. In response to the conflict, the Security Council deployed a small observer force – United Nations Operation in Somalia (UNOSOM I) – to monitor a nominal ceasefire that had been negotiated between Mahdi and Aidid.

UNOSOM I's mandate focused on Mogadishu and its surroundings. It also provided protection for humanitarian-aid deliveries. Aidid's consent to the operation was, however, tenuous at best. Soon enough, Aidid withdrew his consent, to which the Council responded with the deployment of an audacious multinational force to create 'a secure environment'[12] and facilitate humanitarian assistance, under Chapter VII of the UN Charter ('Action with Respect to Threats to the Peace, Breaches of the Peace and Acts of Aggression'). The force was known as the United Task Force (UNITAF), alongside the United States' *Operation Restore Hope*. UNITAF was effective within its limited mandate (relief protection), time frame (three months) and geographical area (40% of the country). After the departure of UNITAF, a second UN Somali mission was deployed in support of the national reconciliation process, which had been concluded in March 1993. UNOSOM II was charged with the creation of a secure environment and the rehabilitation of the political institutions and economy of Somalia. The mission's biggest dilemma, however, was dealing with the disarmament of the various militias.

On 5 June 1993, a Pakistani detachment sent to investigate one of Aidid's weapon caches was attacked and 24 peacekeepers were killed. The council responded with Resolution 837, which effectively declared war on Aidid and made UNOSOM II a peace-enforcement operation. Missions like UNOSOM II rarely begin as peace-enforcement operations, tending to evolve from peacekeeping through a process of mission creep. The basis for the concept of peace enforcement can be found in Article 42 of the UN Charter, but is often ambiguously defined, given the mention of 'all necessary means' – implying the possible use of force at the strategic level. Under a peace-enforcement mandate, the UN gives up its impartiality and seeks to 'conquer the warring factions', 'impose distinct arrangements in the midst of an ongoing war', or 'implement the terms of a comprehensive peace agreement'.[13] It is therefore best to view both peace enforcement and war fighting as one and the same. Under its new peace-enforcement mandate UNOSOM II (along with US Task Force Ranger) launched a series of unsuccessful raids against Aidid's forces, serving only to promote Aidid as a national hero and tarnishing the legitimacy of the UN among the local population. In October, the US Task Force Ranger launched the ill-fated 'Black Hawk Down' raid into central Mogadishu, which resulted in the deaths of 19 servicemen. The event arguably contributed to the US decision to withdraw its forces and eventually the withdrawal of the UN mission in 1995.

After 1999

After the failures in Somalia and Bosnia (as well as in Rwanda), peacekeeping ground to a halt in the mid-1990s, in the middle of 'a vaguely defined no-man's land'.[14] This was largely because, during the early 1990s, doctrinal development simply could not keep pace with the hyperactive nature of deployments. In this context, 1999 was a key year in the history of UN peacekeeping. After the post-1990s retrenchment, the Security Council began to establish a host of new missions: in East Timor (United Nations Transitional Administration in East Timor [UNTAET]); in the DRC (United Nations Organisation Mission in DRC [MONUC]); in Kosovo (United Nations Interim Administration Mission in Kosovo [UNMIK]); and in Sierra Leone (United Nations Mission in Sierra Leone [UNAMSIL]).

At the same time, the Department of Peacekeeping Operations (DPKO) – under Jean-Marie Guéhenno and Lakhdar Brahimi – embarked on an ambitious project, seeking to lay the conceptual groundwork for peacekeeping that was conducted in difficult and non-permissive environments. Such environments were firmly the domains of armed groups. For UN peacekeeping to make a difference, it was argued, a reframing of the concept was required. The results of this project were encapsulated in the 'Report of the Panel on United Nations Peacekeeping' (the Brahimi Report) and 'United Nations Peacekeeping Operations: Principles and Guidelines' (the Capstone Doctrine). The reframing, however, was relatively subtle, with both documents reaffirming the core principles of impartiality, consent and minimum use of force. It was argued that these principles, albeit refashioned, remained the bedrock upon which peace-keeping continues to operate. Brahimi called on the Security Council to authorise missions with mandates that would allow for 'military initiative [to be exercised] in dangerous environments'.[15] For this to occur, Brahimi proposed that the principle of impartiality be redefined under a new rubric, which might be termed active or new impartiality:

> Impartiality for such operations must therefore mean adherence to the principles of the Charter and to the objectives of a mandate that is rooted in those Charter principles. Such impartiality is not the same as neutrality or equal treatment of all parties in all cases for all time, which can amount to a policy of appeasement. In some cases, local parties consist not of moral equals but of obvious aggressors and victims, and peacekeepers may not only be operationally justified in using force but morally compelled to do so.[16]

This new concept of impartiality would, in turn, shape a UN mission's authority to use force. In this vein, it was argued that although the UN did not wage war, the Council should authorise missions with robust rules of engagement to take on spoilers if necessary; this was referred to in Capstone as the use of force at a tactical level – the foundation of robust peacekeeping. Moreover, Capstone posited that UN missions 'can only succeed if the parties on the ground are genuinely committed to resolving the conflict through a political process'.[17] If this commitment did not exist, the Security Council should explore alternatives to deploying a peacekeeping operation. The Council, however, was selective about which stipulations of the Brahimi Report it would adhere to, and those it would ignore.

Several post-Brahimi UN missions illustrate the varied responses of the UN to the context-specific challenges of peace-keeping environments. UN missions after 1999 confronted a new set of threats in non-permissive environments, arguably the most potent being posed by armed groups. To date, the UN has demonstrated a mixed record in addressing these challenges. While robust peacekeeping quickly emerged as a new concept that engendered both the spirit of Brahimi and impartiality, even before the Brahimi Report was handed down in August 2000, the UN had undertaken robust operations, such as against the RUF in Sierra Leone.

Sierra Leone: UNAMSIL

In late April 2000, when the RUF confronted the fledgling UN Mission in Sierra Leone (UNAMSIL), 300 peacekeepers were captured along with their equipment. The incident was hugely embarrassing for the UN; UNAMSIL peacekeepers had abjectly failed to uphold their freedom of movement (FOM), or defend themselves and the mission. By backing down, the peacekeepers not only placed the mission on the brink of collapse, but also served to embolden the RUF. Soon enough, the RUF was advancing on the capital, Freetown. In response to these dramatic events, the UK quickly deployed a sizeable military detachment to reinforce UNAMSIL and evacuate foreign nationals.

Pressure began to mount on the RUF. Following its remarkable failure, UNAMSIL was given a new mandate: 'to deter and, where necessary, counter the RUF by responding robustly to any hostile actions or threat of imminent and direct use of force'.[18] The mission soon tested several of Brahimi's recommendations. In addition to the strengthened mandate, the mission was issued new rules of engagement (ROEs) that enabled it to 'use force, including deadly force, in self-defence against any hostile act or intent'.[19] Secretary-General Kofi Annan went further, declaring in his report to the Security Council that 'the use of force against all elements that continue to display a hostile intent toward the United Nations would be warranted and justified'.[20] This was the first time since 1960 in Katanga that the UN had given one of its missions instructions to respond decisively to hostile 'intent' rather than only when fired upon.

The Security Council also dispatched a mission to Sierra Leone to investigate what had gone wrong in May. The report concluded that:

> Only a sustained and effective military instrument, with the capability to extend its reach throughout the country and following clear political and military objectives, can maintain pressure on the RUF and create incentives for dialogue and disarmament … The combination of firm, proactive peacekeeping, within the flexibility authorized by the resolutions, and the implementation of our broader recommendations can exert a significant impact on a rebellion, many members of which are looking for a road to life without conflict.[21]

Credible military pressure from the UK, Guineans and UNAMSIL led, in part, to greater political engagement by the RUF, which eventually culminated in the signing of the 10 November Abuja Ceasefire.

MONUSCO and the Force Intervention Brigade

In the DRC, MONUC began offensive operations following a period of perceived weakness; the failure to repel the advance of Rally for Congolese Democracy (RCD) rebels on Bukavu in

2004 had discredited MONUC in the eyes of the local population. That event prompted a reorganisation of the mission. An Eastern Division was created and the bulk of MONUC's 20,000 troops were subsumed under this new command structure. In 2006, MONUC was once again tested, this time by the RCD's successor, the CNDP, around Goma. In this case, however, MONUC responded robustly, countering the incursion with attack helicopters and armoured personnel carriers. Numerous fighters were killed and, more importantly, a clear message was sent to the CNDP leadership that such actions would be countered by force (discussed further in Chapter Four).

Yet, in the absence of credible political and disarmament processes, the meagre gains of MONUC's robust action were reversed. The Kivus continued to suffer at the hands of around 40 armed groups, as well as an ill-disciplined and downright abusive army. In mid-2013, an impatient Security Council decided to authorise the establishment of a Force Intervention Brigade (FIB) to conduct offensive operations in an effort to 'neutralise' the negative forces in the Eastern Congo, namely the M23, ADF-Nalu, and FDLR. It marked the first time since the RRF in Bosnia that UN peacekeepers had become a party to the conflict, and by doing so became subject to international humanitarian law (IHL) and the Geneva Conventions.

In practice, the FIB essentially conducted joint-offensive operations, with the Armed Forces of the Democratic Republic of the Congo (FARDC) taking the lead. The FIB's first engagements took place against the M23 over a four-day period in October 2013, and involved the encirclement of M23 positions 'near Kiwanja, Munigi/Kibati and north-west of Rutshuru'[22]. In a coordinated effort, the FARDC and FIB outflanked M23 units, while attack helicopters rocketed hardened defensive positions. The senior leadership quickly understood that their position was untenable, and sought a renegotiated disarmament in Kampala. As of early 2014, MONUSCO made overtures to the effect that the FIB would engage the ADF-Nalu, and, at the insistence of Rwanda, the FDLR. In mid-2014, the Southern African Development Community (SADC) and International Conference on the Great Lakes Region (ICGLR) decided to apply a deadline for FDLR disarmament, promising that a failure to unconditionally surrender would result in the commencement of military action. Unfortunately, regional politicking undermined the FIB's position, with key contributors South Africa and Tanzania clearly lukewarm at the prospect of directly engaging the FDLR. The FIB also had to contend with the 'nuisance'[23] of the ADF-Nalu, which reportedly committed attacks around Beni.

Despite a promising start, both the FIB and MONUSCO underperformed, prompting efforts to re-energise the mission once again.[24] MONUSCO has been hamstrung by the reluctance of Troop Contributing Countries (TCCs) to commit their units to patrol vulnerable areas. It also struggles to achieve cohesion between its more aggressive elements – the FIB – and the main mission. The UN's experiment cannot yet be declared a failure, but the events of 2014 highlighted the problems inherent to stabilisation operations and the dynamics of the use of force in peacekeeping.

UN missions have drawn on myriad strategies to contend with their operating environments around the world; a range of responses made to a range of groups. This chapter has introduced the concept of peace operations in international politics – an expression of complex interaction between host governments, UN staff and diplomats in New York and on the ground. The next chapters will discuss the points of intersection between UN missions and non-state armed groups, examining political strategies, robust peacekeeping and the protection of civilians.

Notes

1 'Resolution 998', *UN General Assembly*.

2 'Mr Human Rights', *The Economist*, 26 December 1992, p. 73.

3 Trevor Findlay, *The Use of Force in UN Peace Operations* (New York: Oxford University Press, 2002), p. 5.

4 *Ibid.*, p. 56.

5 'Resolution 161', *UN Security Council* (reference no: S/RES/161/1961).

6 Alex Morrison, James Kiras and Douglas Fraser, *Peacekeeping with Muscle: The Use of Force in International Conflict Resolution* (Clementsport, NS: Canadian Peacekeeping Press, 1997), p. ix.

7 'Handbook on United Nations Multidimensional Peacekeeping Operations', *Peacekeeping Best Practices Unit* (New York: United Nations, 2003), foreword by Jean-Marie Guéhenno.

8 Alex Bellamy, Paul Williams and Stuart Griffin, *Understanding Peacekeeping, 2nd Edition* (Cambridge: Polity Press, 2010), p. 245.

9 See Boutros Boutros-Ghali, 'An Agenda for Peace: Preventive Diplomacy, Peacemaking and Peace-keeping', http://www. un.org/ga/search/view_doc. asp?symbol=A/47/277.

10 'Resolution 819', *UN Security Council* (reference no: S/RES/819/1993).

11 'Resolution 824', *UN Security Council* (reference no: S/RES/824/1993), clause 4 (a).

12 'Resolution 733', *UN Security Council* (reference no: S/RES/733/1992).

13 Michael Doyle and Nicholas Samabnis, 'Peacekeeping Operations', in Thomas Weiss and Sam Daws (eds), *The Oxford Handbook on the United Nations* (New York: Oxford University Press, 2007), p. 332.

14 See John Ruggie, 'Wandering in the Void: Charting the U.N.'s New Strategic Role', *Foreign Policy*, 1 December 1993, http://www. foreignaffairs.com/articles/49397/ john-gerard-ruggie/wandering-in-the-void-charting-the-uns-new-strategic-role.

15 William Durch and Madeline England, 'The Purposes of Peace Operations', in New York University Center for International Cooperation, *Annual Review of Global Peace Operations 2009* (New York: Lynne Rienner, 2009), p. 42.

16 'Report of the Panel on United Nations Peace Operations', *UN General Assembly* (New York: United Nations, 2000).

17 'United Nations Peacekeeping Operations: Principles and Guidelines', *United Nations* (New York: United Nations, 2008).

18 'Resolution 1313', *UN Security Council* (reference no: S/RES/1313/2000), clause 3 (b).

19 'Fourth Report of the Secretary-General on the United Nations Mission in Sierra Leone', *UN Security Council* (New York: United Nations, 2000), paragraph 89.

20 *Ibid.*

21 'Report of the Security Council Mission to Sierra Leone', *UN Security Council* (New York: United Nations, 2000), p. 13.

22 Darren Oliver, 'Pincer Movements, Choppers and Teamwork: How the M23 was Pushed Back', Think Africa Press, 30 October 2013, http:// thinkafricapress.com/drc/pincer-

movements-choppers-and-team-work-how-m23-was-pushed-back.

23 Albert Kambale, 'Rebels Kill 26 in DRC Machete Attack as UN chief Told to Leave,' AFP, 16 October 2014, http://news.yahoo.com/26-killed-dr-congo-attack-blamed-ugandan-rebels-111552491.html.

24 Louis Charbonneau, 'U.N. Wants Fewer but Better Performing Troops in Congo', Reuters, 5 January 2015, http://www.reuters.com/article/2015/01/05/us-congodemocratic-un-idUSKBN0KE1UI20150105.

CHAPTER THREE

Methods, challenges and opportunities for engagement

Whether it is a light, non-military political mission or a peace-keeping one costing US$1 billion, all UN missions are engaged in a political project. The failures of the past have certainly made policymakers acutely aware of the need for missions to pursue political strategies and have political solutions. Today, 'there can only be a political solution' is the catch-all phrase uttered ad nauseam in most UN press briefings and policy documents. The seminal Brahimi Report, too, notes: 'peacekeeping cannot substitute for an effective political process'.[1]

Nevertheless, in spite of these pronouncements, the concept of the political process – which should constitute the core of every mission – is little understood, chronically understudied and oft-neglected. UN missions have appeared to drift on the ebb and flow of political tides, rather than creating a strong, coherent political project. All peace agreements remain unfinished, and so constant mediation is required on the part of missions to deal with ever-evolving situations. Quite often, the agreement does not adequately address the roots of a conflict – hence a political process is followed, to edge slowly towards solving these issues in their entirety.

In the early 1990s, UN missions, often with the support of a group of friends, constituted the backbone of the international community's efforts towards peace. Missions such as ONUMOZ in Mozambique, UNTAG in Namibia, and ONUSAL in El Salvador were all drivers of the respective country's political processes. SRSGs and UN envoys such as Martti Ahtisaari (for Namibia), Aldo Ajello (for Mozambique), and Álvaro de Soto (for El Salvador) had a direct hand in the mediation of the particular accords, or at the very least in their active verification. Although it is clear that all UN missions are political, the UN today is not always as well positioned to take charge of the political process as it once was, due to the involvement of an ever-growing constellation of new actors. Nevertheless, even with a limited role or mandate, all UN missions should actively and ardently pursue a political project, aimed at addressing the root causes of conflict – both at the national and local levels.

Political process

The term political process can encompass a lot, as Bruce Jones, Jake Sherman and Richard Gowan suggest:

> It … may include ongoing contacts between parties to a peace agreement; a democratic process involving elections or the approval of a constitution; or regional and international contacts on the status of a contested territory. Most UN operations are mandated to protect or sustain one or more such processes, and their utility varies according to the political progress they contribute to.[2]

By way of an agreement between the parties, political processes seek the resolution of conflict by peaceful means, involving a 'mixture of politics, diplomacy, changing relationships, negotiation, mediation, and dialogue in both official and unofficial arenas'. [3] The political process does not, however, begin and end with the agreement. It encompasses the ongoing machinations between key actors, the emergence of new players, and the dynamics of wider society. The most effective political processes aim to not only bring an end to fighting, achieving negative peace (through elite pacts), but also to build a more positive peace, by eliminating the root causes of conflict.

The role of the UN

In a perfect world, UN missions should strive to fill a number of roles in the political process, outlined below.

Custodian

Every UN mission underwrites its respective political process on behalf of the international community. Without the presence of some form of third-party verification, trust usually cannot be adequately built between the parties involved. Stephen Stedman argues that the success or failure of a process hinges on an international custodian's ability to create and implement 'coherent, effective strategies for protecting peace and managing spoilers'. [4] In the majority of cases, UN missions take on the role of international custodian – to help make, keep and build the peace, and sometimes enforce it.

Mediator

Notwithstanding criticisms of the UN's supposed poor performance as a mediator and its apparent lack of 'real political leverage', [5] the fact remains: the UN represents one of the most trusted third parties and an 'attractive [mediator] to many armed groups'. [6] Most often, the UN fulfils a de facto role of

post-agreement mediator – a mix of troubleshooting, medi-
ating the realities of the agreement, and even reforging the
settlement itself. Once UN missions are tethered to a process,
by way of a verification role, some form of political management of the process is inevitable, even if a mission possesses
a limited mandate (the case with the United Nations Mission
in Nepal, for example). For a mission to manage a process, the
role and input of the head of the mission – the SRSG – is crucial.
He or she can empower a mission through effective mediation
or undermine it through impotent mediation attempts. Time
and time again, the leadership has proved to be the make-or-
break component of missions.

Despite their name, comprehensive peace agreements are
rarely comprehensive. More often than not, they paper over
the root causes of conflict. Subsequent agreements need to be
made after the fact, and the words of the agreement need to
be brought to life – and made workable. Over time, the UN
can assist the parties in filling in the blanks, providing clarity
and negotiating the modalities of the UN's work itself. In the
early phases of a process, wildly unrealistic timelines, brought
about by rushed bargains, can present significant roadblocks
in the way of peace. It is also common for peace agreements
to spawn an array of institutions, such as commissions for the
management of the peace; a peace and reconciliation commission; an electoral commission; and even ministries of peace.
Incisive UN missions will seek to resolve the impasses, and
handle the games regularly played out in such fora. Proactive
missions will court controversy and press the parties, while
still maintaining their impartiality, and spend their political
capital when necessary to make progress.

Central to the UN's work as mediator is its ability to iden-
tify the evolving needs of the political process and how the
mission should accommodate them. If a mission feels that it is

in danger of being derailed, the UN might, for example, recognise the need for a fundamental recommitment of the parties to the political process. Looming elections can also exacerbate tensions during a peace process. New constellations of armed groups inevitably emerge to take advantage of substantial power fluctuations, and some of these groups may also need to be included in the process. Accounting for the shifting landscape, through new road maps and new agreements, may be required to place the peace back on track, but it is a task fraught with challenges. In certain complex situations, the UN might be confronted with a patchwork of agreements (for example, bilateral, multi-party, all inclusive, ceasefire, humanitarian access). It is necessary for missions, in these situations, to piece together the peace-agreement jigsaw, and find some level of coherence.[7] Equally, missions may become disempowered when mediation efforts are carried out as a side venture by 'teams separate from the peacekeeping missions, reducing the peacekeepers' leverage'. While this can be constructive in some instances, in others, such an approach 'can be problematic in that political judgments should determine the overarching strategy for UN operations, rather than being on a separate track'.[8]

Interlocutor

UN missions are well positioned, with their vast network of civil-affairs officers and peacekeepers, to open up informal 'channel[s] of communication'[9] with armed groups. For example, in the DRC, 'MONUC military observers and civilian staff were used to liaise with Mai-Mai intermediaries to establish contact with FDLR fighters to facilitate the repatriation of foreign fighters as part of the DDR program'.[10] Negotiating with an armed group on the safe passage of humanitarian aid can be a gateway to engagement on more comprehensive matters.

Guide

Every UN mission acts as a guide to the peace process, enlightening the parties to its various aspects and potential pitfalls. While the parties are likely novices when it comes to pursuing a political process, chances are the UN mission is stocked with expertise – and can therefore draw on relevant know-how gained from other experiences (while avoiding template thinking and recognising that every process is unique). For armed groups to be conformable with the process, they must 'have knowledge of the issues to be negotiated (such as cease-fires), and their implications'.[11] UN missions are not usually in a position to offer capacity-building training for under-resourced armed groups, but a range of other actors regularly provide such training – including the Centre for Humanitarian Dialogue and Berghof Peace Support.

Contingency planner

UN missions must anticipate inevitable ruptures, which risk upending even the most seemingly straightforward political processes. As every peace process encounters hurdles, it is the job of the UN mission to plan for contingencies, predict possible ruptures, and act accordingly to prevent derailment of the process. The Dutch proverb 'the prevention is better than the cure' holds true for UN missions because the cure is almost always costlier in both human and financial terms.[12] Despite all this, UN missions are programmed to be reactive, and seldom draw upon their foresight or act pre-emptively. In Timor Leste (in 2006) and in South Sudan and CAR (in 2013), for example, the respective missions failed to predict foreseeable crises.

Innovator

The UN, as the ultimate bureaucracy, is not an organisation renowned for its creativity. Nevertheless, there have been some notable examples of innovative measures taken in missions, mostly born of personal initiative. UNMIT, under the leadership of Ian Martin, decided to use 111 Nepali ex-soldiers from India as part of an Interim Task Force (ITF) to fill a gap in the monitoring of Maoist Army cantonment sites. Although UN headquarters were not overly enamoured with the idea, the ITF 'became invaluable to the overall monitoring presence at the cantonments'.[13] The United Nations Operation in Mozambique (ONUMOZ), led by Aldo Ajello, proved adept in the management of the political process:

> Rather than simply attempting to re-create organisational routines that had functioned elsewhere, the members of the operation gathered sufficient technical information in Mozambique, defined problems based on local knowledge, coordinated with their counterparts, integrated organisational behaviour with the environment, and exercised creative leadership to avert crises and incrementally alter the actions of the warring parties.[14]

Similarly, ONUSAL – enabled by Alvaro de Soto and led by Iqbal Riza – was a highly adaptable mission, which evolved to match the 'changing demands of the peace process'.[15]

The importance of mediation and the political project cannot be overstated. Lessons learned from previously successful UN missions indicate that their success is largely 'thanks to effective mediation by their civilian leaders rather than simply by their military presence'.[16] The political core of the mission, however, is not always assured, as Lakhdar Brahimi and Salman Ahmed suggest: 'it is easy [for UN missions] to lose sight of the connection between mediation and peacekeeping, once attention shifts to the deployment of military, police and civilian personnel and the individual tasks they are expected to support.'[17]

UN missions need to promote well-crafted political processes that are inclusive of armed groups, but at the same time do not allow them to monopolise the process or 'shoot their way to the negotiating table'.[18]

Engaging armed groups

Reaching out to non-state actors may help the political process become, through inclusivity, more legitimate. It does, however, pose dilemmas concerning the UN's relationship with the state. How the balance is struck, and how it is managed over time, must depend on the specific context. Should UN missions encourage engagement with armed groups? This is a question that continues to confound many missions. Integrating an armed group into a political process scares many governments, as engagement and possible integration are seen as legitimisation of the group. Worse still, bargaining with armed groups (including through the use of amnesties), especially those with a history of violence, opens up governments to charges of complicity (appeasement), and a denial of victims' rights. Although engagement with armed groups might reside in a moral grey area, the alternative – continuing military action – is usually futile, expensive and bloody. Militarists may argue that a decisive military victory makes for a more definitive peace (such as in Sri Lanka). However, it is clear from history that prolonged and often scorched-earth counter-insurgencies have the effect of stirring up a veritable hornet's nest of armed rebels – as the Government of Sudan's Darfur campaign has highlighted.

In the post-Arab Spring world, governments are rightly fearful of non-state challengers – especially those that are armed. This fear has translated into an aversion to meaningful political engagement at the UN level. This is particularly the case since 9/11, with the increased use of the terrorist label to describe groups. It is now common to see the UN openly brandishing its state bias by 'intervening or re-organizing its interventions to protect governments and extend their authority'.[19] Yet, at the same time, armed groups are the central antagonists or protagonists (depending on one's perspective) in most conflicts. They are, therefore, instrumental in the creation of a positive peace. Some argue that any and every group can be negotiated with, regardless of how belligerent they may appear. Others argue that there will always be groups that are irreconcilable, and that these groups should be neutralised. The reality on the ground makes the choice a simple one, despite reticence or misgivings; it becomes a question of not 'whether to engage but how best to engage armed groups'.[20] UN missions, as currently constituted, simply do not possess the military potential to impose a solution by way of a military defeat of an armed group. The application of military force by UN missions against spoilers is likely to remain circumspect, and so UN missions must seek to encourage political engagement.

The role of the UN mission in terms of political engagement should be centred on tackling the root causes of conflict and the grievances that gave rise to it. This can be achieved through the encouragement of tailored political processes that seek to eliminate, or at least address, core concerns of the parties. The logic is that if a political process resolves the main grievances of an armed group, then that group should lose relevance and cease to exist. As a mediator, the UN mission can concentrate on urging armed groups to renounce violence and 'abandon maximalist political demands'.[21] According to Stedman, once a group has given up its maximalist position, it becomes easier for compromises to be made. If a group puts forward a set of non-negotiable demands, the UN can encourage all parties to accommodate and make concessions around these demands. In so doing, inclusion in the political process acts as an inducement for spoilers to cease using violence. However, if a total spoiler is unwilling to abandon its maximalist position, then the political process might be best served by the implementation of a 'departing train strategy': to continue with the planned peace process, irrespective of whether the armed group joins it.[22]

Co-option is another strategy that may be pursued. Co-opting armed groups and their leadership cadres into 'a political setting' can be achieved through 'distributing resources and sharing political responsibility'.[23] This requires integrating the leaders of an armed group into institutional arrangements and power-sharing schemes, and involving them in 'day-to-day politics'.[24] To some degree, co-option provides groups and their leaders with a stake in the peace, tests their commitment to that peace, and holds them accountable to their constituents, as 'even the most selfish leaders are under pressure to deliver – and therefore may be receptive for incentives and guarantees, assured by institutional arrangements'.[25]

In the same breath, the dangers of co-opting armed groups should be considered. The inclusion of armed groups can create distortions and negatively impact on the peace process, if incorrectly handled. In anarchical environments where power, security and ultimate survival are ensured through force of arms, the politics of the gun can win out over a more progressive and representative politics. In post-civil-war climates, the newly minted transitional government lies at the centre of national politics and the economy, hence government constitutes the prize. Jason Stearns explains the phenomenon as it pertains to the DRC: 'in the Congo everything flows from political office: the best business deals, influence, and status.'[26] Likewise, in South Sudan changes made to the constitution in 2011 'rolled back federalism' and centralised power in Juba.

Under these new conditions, the office of the president becomes the 'only position worth competing for since control of the executive amounts to control of the entire political system'.[27] Thus, the conflict between Riek Machar and Salva Kiir was born out of a contest for power at the centre of the state. The forging of a political process in such a scenario, directed by the 'self-serving leadership'[28] of armed groups, can recreate the conditions of exclusivity, allowing for the conflict to replay under another guise. Essentially, there is a monopolisation of the political process by armed groups and the creation of 'a bargaining forum between warlords and predatory leaders'.[29] The political processes of Lome (for Sierra Leone) and the Inter-Congolese Dialogue (in the DRC) are two examples where this occurred.

Sierra Leone

The case of Lomé and the RUF highlights the dangers of warlord governments once unrepresentative armed groups gain power. The peacemaking efforts in Sierra Leone (driven by the US, UK and Nigeria), which culminated in the Lomé Peace Agreement in 1999, effectively elevated, legitimised and recognised the RUF as a credible, trustworthy partner in peace – an assumption that was later proven to be deeply misguided. The RUF was notoriously untrustworthy and enjoyed little popular support – the public was deeply fearful of the group. Moreover, the RUF had failed to live up to two previous agreements: the Abidjan Peace Accord (1996) and the Conakry Peace Plan (1997). Lomé, nevertheless, offered an amnesty and pardon to ex-RUF combatants, granted the RUF a place in the transitional government, and awarded its leader, Foday Sankoh, chairmanship of the Commission for the Management of Strategic Resources, National Reconstruction and Development (CMRRD) – and with it, control of the country's alluvial diamond production. The agreement was plainly an appeasement of the RUF. Instead of pressuring the RUF into a negotiated disarmament, which eventually happened under the Abuja Ceasefire, 'the outside world bestowed legitimacy on it'.[30] With the benefit of hindsight, it is clear that 'the dismantling of the group, rather than its political consolidation, would [have been] of greater benefit to the peacebuilding project'.[31]

DRC

Following the signing of the Lusaka Agreement in 1999 the parties to the Second Congo War agreed to withdraw their forces from the country, and nurture an Inter-Congolese Dialogue (ICD) aimed at creating the conditions for a 'new political dispensation and national reconciliation in the DRC'. For all intents and purposes, the process was intended to forge a political power-sharing agreement between the government, unarmed opposition, civil society and main armed groups: Rally for Congolese Democracy – Goma (RCD-Goma); Rally for Congolese Democracy – National (RCD-N), Rally for Congolese Democracy – Movement for Liberation (RCD-ML); Movement for the Liberation of Congo (MLC); and the Mai-Mai. The three main parties were the government, RDC-Goma and the MLC, with each holding to 'incompatible objectives that largely prevented a compromise'.[32]

After a series of protracted negotiations, the main parties to the conflict signed the Global and All-Inclusive Agreement on the Transition in the DRC in December 2002. Yet, the agreement fell short of addressing the roots of the conflict, and instead largely concentrated on mapping out a power-sharing arrangement (the so-called 1+4 formula) that would see Joseph Kabila retain the presidency through the two-year transition with Azarias Ruberwa (from RCD-Goma) and Jean-Pierre Bemba (from the MLC) holding two of four vice-presidential positions. The ICD was founded on a promising notion: dialogue forged between a cross-section of Congolese society. This style of process 'indicated that the belligerent parties were not considered the only relevant political actors, but that political legitimacy could also be acquired without resorting to violence'.[33] However, at the end of the day, the politics of the gun usurped the inclusivity of the dialogue. In effect, 'the implied logic of this process – granting insurgents political power in order to quell their insurgencies – persists until today, creating incentives for elites to mobilize armed groups'.[34] Armed groups and their controlling elites are attracted to the prospect that armed rebellion could be used to gain political power.

Negotiated disarmament

Are all armed groups that commit themselves to a political process entitled to a stake in the outcome of that process? As discussed above, armed groups that possess the means of violence hold political power. However, this does not necessarily mean that transitional arrangements should be inclusive of all armed groups. As the case of the RUF indicated, handing political power to armed groups can represent a dangerous appeasement (namely, buying peace rather than building it). A clear and credible alternative to allowing armed groups a stake in the transition is negotiated disarmament, made possible by a credible disarmament, demobilisation and reintegration (DDR) programme. The overarching aim of DDR is to ensure that armed groups, which 'have prospered during the active phase of hostilities do not return to the battlefield or find other ways of undermining local and international efforts to build lasting peace, and to do so by finding ways of integrating ex-combatants into the social, economic and political life of post-war society'.[35] Integration, however, cannot amount to a mere bribe to keep former combatants 'busy or out of trouble'.[36] Instead,

Table 1: **The Push and Pull of DDR**

Push: towards armed groups	Pull: away from armed groups
• Cold response from the community	• Good reception upon return
• Lack of employment opportunities	• Family relations
• Lack of a genuine political process	• Internal splits
• Indoctrination and limited information outside group	• Lost cause
	• Intense military pressure
• Indictment (International Criminal Court or national court)	• Constant risk of harm and conflict with host communities
• Fear of the 'unknown'	• Military fatigue
• Peer pressure and fringe benefits	• Useful external communication flows
• Purpose	
• Security	

integration should be seen as an investment in the potential productive employment of ex-combatants.

These fighters are potential agents of insecurity, but, if integrated into security services or reintegrated into society, can become productive members of the community. A carefully calibrated DDR programme serves to provide that transformative function. Yet, in many cases, the sheer number of former combatants overwhelms underfunded DDR efforts; from 75,000 (in Sierra Leone) to 330,000 combatants (in the DRC). DDR must be tailored to suit each armed group, so it is important to understand how each group retains its individual fighters – the push and pull factors (see Table 1). With these factors in mind, the appropriate incentives can be provided to effectively entice individuals into the DDR programme.

Reintegration

Arguably, the most salient challenge to any peace process is the comprehensive reintegration of ex-combatants into the social, economic and political life of the community. Creating decent employment opportunities for former combatants is particularly challenging; the labour market is often simply not able to adequately absorb new entrants. Compounding the issue is the fact that the majority of ex-combatants lack education, employable skills and start-up capital, and often carry the stigma of conflict with them as they return to their home communities. At the same time, ex-combatants represent a wealth of human capital, which, if tapped correctly, can yield significant development and security benefits.[38] This can be achieved through local labour-intensive employment initiatives (infrastructure, reconstruction and agriculture) and employability programmes (skills development and training).

DDR programmes have exhibited an unfortunate tendency to create distortions in the local economy, as they are often the 'only [economic] game in town'.[39] They should, instead, manage the expectations of former combatants and seek to fill the gaps communities and the private sector have, whilst avoiding the oversupply of certain skill sets. Moreover, as ex-combatants emerge from an armed-group structure, they are confronted with a high degree of uncertainty about the future. It is, therefore, necessary for reintegration programmes to tap into 'networks of support (social and economic) that serve as alternatives to the armed group'.[40]

Integration into armed services

The integration of members of disbanded armed groups into the national armed services is a practice regularly undertaken after the conclusion of peace agreements. The integration of ex-combatants into the national military is often a condition of an agreement, as integration provides leaders and their members a stake in the peace – and a host of other benefits. The promise of integration, however, can embolden leaders to leverage their position (returning to the battlefield or bolstering their group members). Once integrated, a new set of challenges can emerge, all of which run counter to the principles of military cohesion, rank harmonisation and right sizing.[41] The FARDC is a cautionary tale highlighting the potential pitfalls of integration.

In 2003, Laurent Nkunda of the RCD-Goma refused to integrate into FARDC, the country's new army. The RCD, although popular within the Rwandan Congolese communities of the Kivus, was deeply unpopular across the rest of the country, which was later reflected in the 2006 election, in which it gained only 15 out of 500 seats. A new insurgency emerged following the election, 'partly in reaction to this loss of power'.[42] Backed by Rwanda, the CNDP, led by Nkunda, laid claim to parts of North Kivu. After a number of incursions and a failed attempt to capture Goma in 2006, Nkunda committed the CNDP to a process known as 'mixage' – integrating CNDP combatants into the regular army. The process gave Nkunda authority over five brigades, which allowed him to assert control over a greater region of the country. Following the splintering of the group and the rise of Bosco Ntaganda, the group then committed to an agreement signed in March 2009. The agreement again allowed CNDP combatants to be integrated into the national army, and again these units later rebelled to form a new group known as M23. It is clear from the brief narrative of the RCD-Goma, CNDP and M23 that 'by repeatedly integrating armed groups into the FARDC, the government has not only provided incentives for further insurrection, it has effectively sanctioned impunity'.[43]

Mismanaged integration of armed groups into a national military structure can have a host of negative repercussions, not the least of which are the types of rebellion witnessed in the DRC. Poorly managed integration, characterised by inadequate retraining and management of the military, can weaken the cohesion of the army and create parallel command structures based on previously developed loyalties. The process of mixage in the DRC, for instance, resulted in brigades that 'were dominated by a majority of up to 75 per cent from a single former armed group – leading to separate chains of command within the military, the undermining of central command, and a weaker government grip on the army in the Kivus'.[44]

Remobilisation or recycling of combatants

Remobilising combatants has the potential to set back a political process or, alternatively, spread conflict to another country. Simply put, 'if the grievances and frustrations of demobilized combatants are not addressed through a reintegration strategy, former combatants can be remobilized easily and pose security risks at a regional level.'[45] For some fighters, wartime life becomes the status quo; as one Lebanese Shia militia member was quoted as saying: 'war is my only friend. It's like my wife, I love it. In peace I feel afraid.'[46] Moreover, combatants have developed a set of fighting skills that are not usually applicable to civilian life. The uncomfortable uncertainty of reintegration presents ex-combatants with a challenge, while remobilisation offers the path of least resistance – a way of reclaiming a sense of purpose and power.

In the DRC, the Raia Mutomboki drew in demobilised Mai-Mai as the group's reach expanded from Shabunda to Kalehe. Within a short space of time, remobilised Mai-Mai fighters had become the 'backbone of the movement'. Jason Stearns et al. have come to the conclusion that 'the lack of any real and sustained effort at reintegration has made the Raia Mutomboki an attractive alternative for demobilized Mai-Mai and RCD combatants'.[47] Reintegration must be tailored to break the cycle of mobilisation, and reduce the attractiveness of remobilisation with another group. In the case of Raia Mutomboki, this would require a more holistic approach that would seek to deal with the group's fundamental drivers: the existence of security vacuums, land and customary conflicts, 'and a political logic prevalent among elites, whereby armed groups are used for political influence and leverage'.[48]

The reality is that, in most situations, imperfect agreements are forged from the untidy compromises made around the negotiating table. Elite pacts are clearly necessary in almost every context, but there is also an oft-neglected need to balance these pacts against initiatives designed to address the root causes of the conflict. Indeed, there is an emerging recognition among UN practitioners of the latter's importance.[49] Political processes must, therefore, seek to deal with not only the symptoms of conflict – the emergence of powerful interests and armed groups – but also the underlying drivers of conflict.

Notes

1 NYU Center for International Cooperation, *Building on Brahimi: Peacekeeping in an Era of Strategic Uncertainty* (New York: NYU CIC, 2009), p. 9.

2 *Ibid.*

3 Harold H. Saunders, 'Prenegotiation and Circum-negotiation: Arenas of the Multilevel Peace Process', *Turbulent Peace* (Washington DC: US Institute of Peace, 2001), p. 483.

4 Stephen John Stedman, 'Spoiler Problems in Peace Processes', *International Security*, vol. 22, no. 2, Autumn 1997, p. 6.

5 Saadia Touval, 'Why the UN Fails: It Cannot Mediate', *Foreign Policy*, September–October 1994, p. 46.

6 Teresa Whitfield, *Engaging Armed Groups: Dilemmas and Options for Mediators* (Geneva: Centre for Humanitarian Dialogue, 2010), p. 9.

7 In the Congo, a suite of peace agreements have been signed since the initial Lusaka Peace Agreement in 1999: the Sun City Agreement (as part of the All-Inclusive Process), Kampala Agreement, Pretoria Agreement, and Goma and Nairobi processes.

8 NYU Center for International Cooperation, *Building on Brahimi*, p. 9.

9 Teresa Whitfield, *Engaging Armed Groups*, p. 9.

10 Kelvin Ong, *Managing Fighting Forces: DDR in Peace Processes* (Washington DC: USIP, 2012), p. 26.

11 *Ibid.*, p. 32.

12 Carnegie Commission on Preventing Deadly Conflict, *Preventing Deadly Conflict: Final Report with Executive Summary* (New York: Carnegie Corporation of New York, 1998).

13 Ian Martin, 'The 2008 Constituent Assembly Election: Social Inclusion for Peace', in Sebastian von Einsiedel, David Malone and Suman Pradhan (eds), *Nepal in Transition: From People's War to Fragile Peace* (New York: Cambridge University Press, 2012), p. 209.

14 Lise Morjé Howard, *UN Peacekeeping in Civil Wars* (Cambridge: Cambridge University Press, 2008), pp. 179–80.

[15] See 'Understanding Peacekeeping – Additional Case Studies: ONUSAL', Alex Bellamy and Paul Williams, http://www.polity.co.uk/up2/casestudy/ONUSAL_case_study.pdf.

[16] NYU Center for International Cooperation, *Building on Brahimi*, citing Lise Morjé Howard, *UN Peacekeeping in Civil Wars*.

[17] Lakhdar Brahimi and Salman Ahmed, 'In Pursuit of Sustainable Peace: the Seven Deadly Sins of Mediation', in NYC Center for International Cooperation (ed.), *Robust Peacekeeping: The Politics of Force* (New York: NYC CIC, 2009), p. 56.

[18] Eric Rogier, 'The Inter-Congolese Dialogue: A Critical Overview', in Mark Malan and Joao Gomes Porto (eds), *Challenges of Peace Implementation: The UN Mission in the Democratic Republic of the Congo* (Johannesburg/Pretoria: Institute of Security Studies, 2003), p. 39.

[19] Bruce Jones, 'Preface', in NYC Center for International Cooperation (ed.), *Robust Peacekeeping: The Politics of Force*, p. i.

[20] Conciliation Resources, *Choosing to Engage: Armed Groups and Peace Processes* (London: Conciliation Resources, 2009), p. 1.

[21] Claudia Hofmann and Ulrich Schneckener, 'Engaging Non-State Armed Actors in State- and Peacebuilding: Options and Strategies', *International Review of the Red Cross*, vol. 93, no. 883, September 2011, p. 9.

[22] Stephen John Stedman, 'Spoiler Problems in Peace Processes', p. 15.

[23] Claudia Hofmann and Ulrich Schneckener, 'Engaging Non-State Armed Actors in State- and Peacebuilding: Options and Strategies', p. 9.

[24] *Ibid.*

[25] *Ibid.*, p. 10.

[26] Jason Stearns, *Dancing in the Glory of Monsters: The Collapse of the Congo and the Great War of Africa* (New York: PublicAffairs, 2012), p. 330.

[27] See Hillary Matfess, 'The Root of South Sudan's Crisis is Constitutional not Ethnic', Think Africa Press, 13 May 2014, http://thinkafricapress.com/south-sudan/constitutional-crisis-not-ethnic-one-kiir-machar-splm.

[28] Jakkie Cilliers and Julia Schuenemann, 'The Future of Intrastate Conflict in Africa: More Violence or Greater Peace?', Institute of Security Studies Paper, no. 246, 15 May 2013, p. 5.

[29] Eric Rogier, 'The Inter-Congolese Dialogue: A Critical Overview', p. 39.

[30] Eric G. Berman and Melissa T. Labonte, 'Sierra Leone', in William Durch (ed.), *Twenty -First-Century Peace Operations* (Washington DC: United States Institute of Peace, 2006), p. 143.

[31] Mats Berdal and David Ucko, 'Introduction: The political integration of armed groups after war' in Mats Berdal and David Ucko (eds), *Reintegrating Armed Groups After Conflict* (Milton Park: Routledge, 2009), p. 6.

[32] Eric Rogier, 'The Inter-Congolese Dialogue: A Critical Overview', p. 30.

[33] *Ibid.*, p. 38.

[34] Jason Stearns, Judith Verweijen and Maria Eriksson Baaz, *The National Army and Armed Groups in the Eastern Congo: Untangling the*

Gordian Knot of Security (London/ Nairobi: The Rift Valley Institute, 2013), p. 8.

35 Mats Berdal and David Ucko, 'Introduction: the political integration of armed group after war', p. 2.

36 Mark Knight and Alpaslan Ozerdem, 'Guns, Camps and Cash: Disarmament, Demobilization and Reinsertion of Former Combatants in Transitions from War to Peace', *Journal of Peace Research*, vol. 41, no. 4, July 2004, p. 513.

37 Conciliation Resources, *Choosing to Return: Challenges Faced by the Lord's Resistance Army's Middle-Ranking Commanders* (London: Conciliation Resources, 2009).

38 ILO Programme for Crisis Response and Reconstruction, *Socio-Economic Reintegration of Ex-Combatants* (Geneva: International Labour Organisation, 2009).

39 Robert Muggah, 'No Magic Bullet: A Critical Perspective on Disarmament, Demobilization and Reintegration (DDR) and Weapons Reduction in Post-conflict Contexts', *Round Table*, vol. 94, no. 379, April 2005, p. 246.

40 Eric Shibuya, *Demobilizing Irregular Forces* [Kindle] (Cambridge: Polity Press, 2012).

41 Lesley Anne Warner, 'Armed-Group Amnesty and Military Integration in South Sudan', *RUSI Journal*, vol. 158, no. 6, December 2013.

42 Jason Stearns, Judith Verweijen and Maria Eriksson Baaz, *The National Army and Armed Groups in the Eastern Congo*, p. 23.

43 *Ibid.*

44 *Ibid.*, p. 52.

45 Mark Knight and Alpaslan Ozerdem, 'Guns, Camps and Cash: Disarmament, Demobilization and Reinsertion of Former Combatants in Transitions from War to Peace', p. 502.

46 Stathis Kalyvas, *The Logic of Violence in Civil War* (Cambridge: Cambridge University Press, 2006) citing Michael Johnson, *All Honourable Men: The Social Origins of War in Lebanon* (London: I.B. Tauris, 2001), p. 203.

47 Jason Stearns et al., *Raia Mutomkoki: The Flawed Peace Process in the DRC and the Birth of an Armed Franchise* (London & Nairobi: Rift Valley Institute, 2013), p. 48.

48 *Ibid.*, p. 45.

49 See 'DR Congo: Amid Military Gains, Root Causes of Violence Must Be Addressed, Says UN Official', UN News Centre, 31 January 2014, http://www.un.org/apps/news/story.asp?NewsID=47058&Cr=democratic&Cr1=congo#. UxVtSPSSwag.

CHAPTER FOUR

Role and development of robust peacekeeping

On 24 November 2006, a businessman in the DRC delivering fuel to the CNDP was shot dead by a group of police who had been manning a checkpoint outside of Sake in North Kivu. Soon after the incident, the CNDP's emotionally charged leader Laurent Nkunda mobilised his forces and attacked Sake. After taking the town, he turned his attention towards Goma, the provincial capital. In response, MONUC issued an ultimatum, threatening to use force unless the CNDP ceased offensive operations. Nkunda continued his advance but he was quickly cut off by MONUC, which then used attack helicopters and armour to engage the CNDP just outside Sake. The armed group suffered a significant tactical defeat and over 150 of its fighters were killed. Within three days, Nkunda and the government began negotiations that resulted in an agreement on army integration, or mixage (as detailed in Chapter Three). The UN's robust engagement to protect civilians in Goma stood in stark contrast to the events of Bukavu in 2004. Then, MONUC had issued a similar ultimatum to the RCD (the precursor to the CNDP, led by Nkunda) as it advanced on Bukavu, but it backed down at the last minute. Peacekeepers looked on as the group captured Bukavu and its airport. Approximately 16,000 women were raped during the early stages of the RCD's occupation; 'this city is yours for three days', Nkunda ordered. MONUC's failure to defend Bukavu was disastrous, resulting in a backlash against the mission. Large numbers of Congolese demonstrated in major towns and cities across the country.

As has been illustrated, the emerging concept of robust peacekeeping has been applied in an episodic fashion – in the siege of Sarajevo (1995), Eastern Slavonia (1996), Sierra Leone (2000), Haiti (2005), Côte d'Ivoire (2011) and Eastern Congo (2006). When examining each of these cases, it becomes clear that the practice of robust peacekeeping is more of a 'product of specific conditions and personalities rather than a deliberate expansion of UN strategy and therefore reflecting a lack of coherence and consistency in UN peacekeeping's understanding and application of force'.[1]

Both the Brahimi and Capstone reports advocated the notion that peacekeepers must be made capable of 'defending themselves, other mission components and the mission's mandate, with robust rules of engagement, against those who renege on their commitments to a peace accord or otherwise seek to undermine it by violence'.[2] It was felt that UN missions were too soft and needed to be given the conceptual basis to 'confront the lingering forces of war and violence, with the ability and determination to defeat them'.[3] In other words, UN missions had to become more robust and more proactive.

Efforts to articulate a defined concept, however, never really took flight, and so the idea of robustness has remained just that – an idea. This chapter seeks to address this conceptual gap and render clarity on robust peacekeeping. Essentially, robust peacekeeping involves the use of military pressure (that is, the use of force) to deter or coerce a spoiler (invariably an armed group) into ceasing offensive military operations and/or civilian victimisation. Its overarching aim is to create conditions on the ground conducive to the establishment of negative peace (the mere absence of war) or a minimum level of security (protection of civilians), upon which a more sustainable form of peace and security can be based. It is argued that the practice of robust peacekeeping should be driven by the needs of hard security and the realisation of a political end state. Indeed, if robust peacekeeping is to prove effective, UN missions must be careful to calibrate robust operations with the mission's broader political objectives, and as part of a coherent strategy involving the coordination of other lines of effort – the political process, DDR, Security Sector Reform (SSR), institution-building and governance-reform programmes.

Yet, rather than considering robust peacekeeping as a new form of peacekeeping, this chapter argues that the concept be normalised in non-permissive environments. For this to occur, UN missions need to be engendered with a robustness of posture, only achievable once certain constraints on force commanders specifically, and the department (DPKO) more generally, are lifted.

Levels of intervention and the functions of the military component

In order to build an applicable concept of robust peacekeeping, it is necessary to begin at the level of the Security Council – the strategic level. Before every mission is mandated, the Security Council must determine the level of intervention it is prepared to permit (Chapter VI or Chapter VII). It is true that all peacekeepers 'alter the dynamics and calculations of those in proximity'.[4] Nevertheless, under Chapter VI, UN forces are not expected to change the security situation, while they are under Chapter VII.

UN missions authorised under Chapter VI are not permitted to use force beyond self-defence. Chapter VI implies non-interventionist passivity, demonstrated in traditional inter-positional peacekeeping, involving observation and monitoring of agreements and ceasefires. Chapter VII, on the other hand, implies an active approach on the part of the mission to establish a set of facts on the ground conducive to negative peace (the mere absence of war) and security. As many missions today operate in non-permissive environments (in CAR, the DRC, South Sudan, Darfur and Mali), the Council commonly authorises mandates under Chapter VII.

How do missions implement their Chapter VII mandate? In his book *The Unity of Force*, Rupert Smith, former UN commander general, assesses what military forces can realistically achieve. According to Smith, once deployed, the military can function in four ways. Firstly, it can ameliorate civilian suffering by providing humanitarian relief. Secondly, it can contain violence and so prevent horizontal escalation. Thirdly, it can coerce or deter armed groups. Finally, it can neutralise them, destroying their ability to achieve their political purpose.[5]

Under Chapter VI, peacekeepers function to ameliorate the situation; hence the issuance of limited ROEs, which restrict the use of force to conditions of self-defence. Under Chapter VII, and robust peacekeeping, the military component of the mission functions to deter and coerce. UN missions operating in this way should, therefore, theoretically adopt a threatening posture in order to maximise deterrence. Here, there is a distinct difference between mere deployment of forces (in order to deter) and employment of those forces (in order to coerce). In the DRC, the FIB was authorised under Chapter VII to neutralise armed groups. Whereas robust peacekeeping functions to deter and coerce, the FIB, as a peace-enforcement operation, functions to neutralise: to destroy enemies.

Adherence to principle

Robust peacekeeping, however, is not war fighting, counter-insurgency or peace enforcement. As retired lieutenant-general Babacar Gaye has suggested, 'it may look like war but it's peacekeeping'.[6] Undoubtedly, when missions are engaged in robust peacekeeping, they are operating in a grey conceptual space. The question is whether they can remain true to their guiding principles,and whether it is even important to remain principled.

Impartiality

According to Dag Hammarskjöld, the UN should not be 'used to enforce any specific political solution of pending problems or to influence the political balance decisive to such a solution'.[7] After the crises of the early 1990s, however, the Brahimi and Capstone reports sought to reframe impartiality, noting the limitations of a passive response:

> Impartiality for United Nations operations must therefore mean adherence to the principles of the Charter: where one party to a peace agreement clearly and incontrovertibly is violating its terms, continued equal treatment of all parties by the United Nations can in the best case result in ineffectiveness and in the worst may amount to complicity with evil.[8]

The reports attempted to conceptually separate robust peacekeeping from peace enforcement, rather than simply accepting that 'there is no neat division' between the two.[9] The argument that the UN can 'clinically apply force to manipulate the behaviour of various parties on the ground *without* designating an enemy while simultaneously assuming that such action will not influence the political dynamics of the conflict, is seriously to underestimate the impact of outside military action on the local balance of military, political and economic interests'.[10] Armed groups that are tactically defeated by UN forces will be militarily and politically disadvantaged by such robust actions. UN forces engaged in robust peacekeeping are, therefore, necessarily reshaping the local military and political balance of power – it would be false to claim otherwise. Even if not designated an enemy of the UN, spoilers will likely come to view the UN as a threat, and will act accordingly.

The application of the impartial use of force is desirable but not always possible. Still, every UN mission should endeavour to take on an 'umpire' role – placing itself above the parties, not between them. Equally important, this type of active impartiality should empower and safeguard the political process, namely the rules of the game. The use of force should therefore be applied pragmatically, based on the likelihood that force will change the intentions of spoiler groups. This will depend primarily on how susceptible the group appears to military pressure, as well as the constraints of the mission (see below).

Minimum use of force

Force should be used decisively to achieve tactical objectives, within a strategic framework. If a UN force conducting robust peacekeeping is to sustain its deterrent value, then the mission might have to move beyond minimum necessary force. Instead, the force commander and his contingent commanders should be empowered to judiciously use the level of force deemed appropriate to achieve specific objectives.

Determining the right level of force in peacekeeping, however, is incredibly difficult. The standard rules of engagement (ROEs) offer some clarity; any force must be limited in its intensity and duration, to that which is necessary to achieve the authorised objective. Force should be commensurate to the level of threat, though, in some circumstances, the level of force used may exceed the level of the threat to ensure an authorised objective is achieved. Moreover, during the initial stages of deployment, a strong display of force might be required to, firstly, set back a spoiler and, secondly, project credible deterrence. By using the appropriate level of force at this junction, the UN mission would negate the need to continually reapply force. David Richards recounts that his troops were most effective when they 'had – to coin a phrase – clouted not dribbled… we had gone in hard like we meant it and it had paid dividends'.[11] UN forces should be encouraged to apply military force confidently, or not at all.

Consent

Whose consent is required? All parties to the conflict, or just those parties whose leaders have signed the peace agreement, or only the host government? What if there is no peace agreement, or the agreement is a dead letter, or if there is peace in the making?

UN missions must maintain the consent of the host government, at least on some level. For example, the United Nations African Union Hybrid Mission in Darfur (UNAMID) in Sudan technically operates with the consent of the Government of Sudan (GoS), even if the mission is sorely limited by the government's obstructionism.

In a perfect world, a UN mission would also enjoy the consent of all armed groups (or non-host-government actors) involved in the conflict or peace process. In reality, however, UN missions never enjoy the consent of all parties, especially spoilers operating on the margins of the peace, who have little to gain and much to lose from any form of UN-supported peace process. UN missions should, therefore, be prepared 'to work with partial absence of consent and should be prepared to deal with decayed consent'.[12] Of course, UN missions cannot engage the central parties of the peace agreement if they withdraw their consent and return to the battlefield. As Jean-Marie Guéhenno suggests, UN missions 'must take on violent local challenges to peace implementation, but only at the margins of a peace process. Should the core of that process lose cohesion, a multinational operation will itself have insufficient cohesion – and likely insufficient military strength – to make the center hold.'[13] The response of UN mission leaders to violence by non-consenting groups will depend on a number of factors: for example, whether the group is central to the peace agreement or resides at the fringes of the peace, if the group is engaged in mass atrocity crimes, and if the group enjoys widespread popular support.

The decision to engage a non-consenting party is a singularly difficult one to make – but can lead to positive outcomes. In Sierra Leone, for instance, the Security Council chose to directly confront the RUF rebels, even though the group was party to the bilateral Lomé peace agreement. Subsequent robust action by UNAMSIL led to a renewed ceasefire agreement, and a marked decline in violence.

Robustness: the concept

As already mentioned, when undertaking robust peacekeeping, UN missions operate under Chapter VII, which permits them to judiciously apply the use of force for deterrence and coercion. This recognises that, in the conduct of robust peacekeeping, military force can bring about conditions on the ground conducive to security and negative peace. As also discussed, the basis for robust peacekeeping is a strong presence, posture and profile (PPP): a hardening of the UN's peacekeeping image. From this basis, it is possible to articulate a more detailed explanation of the concept of robustness.

Robust peacekeeping aims to persuade a spoiler to cease its offensive military operations or civilian victimisation by drawing a 'red line'. As the leader of a UN transitional administration deployed to East Timor in 1999, the SRSG, Sergio Vieira de Mello felt it was vital to signal firm intent, on the basis that militants would exploit any perceived weakness:

> We chose not to opt for the usual and classical peacekeeping approach: taking abuse, taking bullets, taking casualties and not responding with enough force, not shooting to kill. The UN had done that before and we weren't going to repeat it here.[14]

In the first instance, the UN force provides an ultimatum and tries to deter spoilers by threatening the use of force. In the event of non-compliance, the UN is required to follow through on its threat, and use force coercively to achieve its objectives. The ultimate aim of UN forces is to create the expectation for an armed group that the costs of non-compliance would be too high to reasonably accept.

At its heart, robust peacekeeping operates on the assumption that, when hard-headed spoilers are confronted by a determined and robust UN force, they will inevitably choose the more amenable option: the negotiating table. It would, however, be naïve in the extreme to suggest that a 'short, sharp shock' would automatically bring all spoilers to the table. Clearly, if spoilers choose to retaliate against the local population or escalate the fight, then UN forces must be prepared to decisively counter such an attack.

Military power assures political and bargaining power. Once the parties to a conflict finally agree to sit down at the negotiating table, the party deemed stronger militarily will have the stronger hand to play. If, then, a UN force inflicts casualties on a spoiler during a tactical engagement, the latter's military capacity will be reduced, resulting in a commensurate decline in the spoiler's potential bargaining power. UN forces must, therefore, be adept in the communication of ultimatums and application of force, so as to place spoilers in a no-win situation. Under these conditions, the negotiating table would appear a more inviting option than the prospect of further tactical confrontation with UN forces.

The ultimatum forms a central element of robust peace-keeping. An effective ultimatum must comprise five elements: clear articulation of the demand (i.e. disarm or cease military activity); the options for compliance (i.e. commit to the political process or DDR programme); a credible threat (i.e. the use of force); the inevitability of follow-through in the event of non-compliance; and a specific time limit. A spoiler must, therefore, be made fully aware of the terms of an ultimatum, and the potential ramifications of non-compliance, as well as the alter-natives open to them, including political engagement and negotiated disarmament (or DDR). Crucially, a UN mission should not issue an ultimatum if its military component is not prepared or willing to follow through: 'never make promises that one cannot keep, or threats that one cannot carry out'.[15]

In the event of non-compliance, the UN's military power should be brought to bear against a spoiler, in as decisive a way as possible (within the bounds of proportionality). The selection of targets, in particular, can be made to alter a deci-sion-maker's mind and leverage the compliance of a spoiler. There are several ways this can be achieved.

Firstly, like a conventional army, armed groups are sustained through their supply lines. Studies estimate that the costs of starting an armed group lie somewhere between US$67,500 and US$450,000 (per 1,000 combatants), while sustaining such a group, in a low-intensity campaign, costs between US$2.6

million and US$16.2m a year.[16] UN forces should undertake interdiction operations aimed at disrupting and/or destroying supply lines, weapons caches and income streams of spoiler groups. Informed by credible intelligence, interdiction can be an effective low-risk method for suffocating a spoiler, as pressure is applied through denial rather than direct confrontation.

Secondly, and most commonly, UN forces can use their military function to deny a spoiler an objective. In the past, UN forces have positioned themselves between a spoiler and his objective (for example, a city or strategic location).

Thirdly, UN forces can target command-and-control (C2) nodes, in order to induce a sense of loss of control, as well as general C2 paralysis and disorganisation, among the armed group. The effectiveness of this method of targeting depends largely on the C2 structure of an armed group. Fourthly, the targeting of an armed group's prize possessions – which might include weapons caches and materiel vehicles (technicals, armored vehicles and supply trucks) – not only degrades military potential, but also produces a psychological effect.

Robustness in practice: Operation Palliser *and Lungi Lol*
Robustness can yield great benefits. After UK forces deployed to Sierra Leone, a Pathfinder Platoon (16 Air Assault Brigade) secured the area around Lungi – a strategic location near Freetown airport – and took up defensive positions. In the early hours of 17 May 2000 they engaged an RUF force numbering in the hundreds (although other sources state figures of 30–40) that had approached the village. The engagement was relatively short, but proved decisive. The RUF suffered significant casualties and withdrew after losing 14–30 of its fighters. With the action at Lungi Lol, *Operation Palliser* established its credibility and deterrent power. Brigadier David Richards later remarked that British forces had 'played a psychological game

and won…we relied on convincing the RUF that they would lose in any confrontation with us… They became disillusioned and disorganised.'[17]

Presence, posture and profile

The concept of presence, posture and profile (PPP) is the cornerstone of robust peacekeeping. A UN force undertaking robust peacekeeping must be able to project its presence and appear stronger and more determined than the opposition, but also be able to engage with the community on a meaningful level. PPP intends to assist military forces determine their 'attitude, deportment, and level of security'[18] in any given situation. All the elements of PPP influence the way a UN force is perceived by both spoilers and the local population.

Firstly, the mere presence or absence of peacekeepers influences the deployment environment, as well as the actors (their actions, perceptions and intentions) in this environment. The impact of mere presence cannot be underestimated. Moreover, deploying to the right place at the right time can have a deterrent effect, adding credibility to messages being delivered through other channels.[19]

Secondly, profile denotes the footprint of the force: whether it is light or heavy. Due to limited troop numbers, UN forces need to utilise their profile to give the intended perception to spoilers and the local population. Likewise, 'the public profile of commanders at all levels also impacts perceptions, and their role must be analysed and opportunities used to transmit key messages.'[20] It is therefore necessary for the mission to be transparent in messaging strategies, in order to communicate to armed groups the PPP of the UN force.

Thirdly, the posture of peacekeepers is demonstrative of both commitment and intent. In essence, posture is another term for the body language of the force, and for peacekeepers their posture should indicate that the UN is not to be trifled with. A smart UN force will obviously adjust its PPP to suit the context: for example, appearing menacing or reassuring; projecting a light or a heavy footprint; being present or not. The practices of the United Nations Transitional Administration for Eastern Slavonia, Baranja and Western Sirmium (UNTAES) in Croatia, and the Australian Contingent (*Operation Solace*) of the Unified Task Force (UNITAF) in Somalia, as well as the afore-mentioned *Operation Palliser* in Sierra Leone, can serve as a guide to the potential robust component of PPPs.

UNTAES

Under the transitional administrator, Jacques Paul Klein, the mission presented itself as a no-nonsense peacekeeping force with a 'robust reputation',[21] capable of effectively engaging with the local population. UNTAES's robust posture was enabled by the deployment of over 5,000 personnel (troops, observers and police). Moreover, the troops were well armed and equipped, with Belgian, Russian and Jordanian mechanised infantry battalions; a Polish Commando Unit; an Argentine Recon company; 70 main battle tanks; 204 armoured personnel carriers; six 155mm howitzers; 24 mortars; an anti-tank company; and a squadron of Ukrainian M-24 attack helicopters.[22]

By all appearances, the force was capable of deterring any threat to the peace and stability of Eastern Slavonia, and was able to draw on the considerable deterrent strength of NATO's Implementation Force (IFOR) stationed in neighbouring Bosnia. For the most part, the idea was to 'keep the tanks and howitzers in the background; the remaining forces were used in patrols and other operations designed to be seen by the local population … specific efforts were made to ensure that such demonstrations were not perceived by the local Serbs as to be threatening to them, but rather as a readiness and willingness by UNTAES to maintain security from external threats and in support of internal law and order.'[23] Not only was UNTAES deployed in sufficient strength, but more importantly, the force was employed against the Arkan's Tigers and Scorpions para-military units. In May 1996, the UNTAES's military component was instructed to take the Djeletovic oilfields from the Serb Chetnik paramilitary group – the Scorpions. Early on 14 May, the force commander's chief of staff was sent to the oilfields to deliver an ultimatum to the group's leader: to depart the area by the afternoon or UNTAES would 'take possession by force'.[24] The ultimatum was backed by a viable show of force with tanks and attack helicopters displayed. The Scorpions weighed their options and were, after a delay, eventually escorted by UNTAES into Serbia. Despite a seemingly peaceful conclu-sion, the Scorpions returned in successive evenings to test the resolve of UNTAES in the vicinity of the oilfield. In response, the Jordanian battalion stationed in the area employed force to neutralise the remaining Scorpions, and restore security.

Operation Solace

In December 1992, within the broader UNITAF mission, the 1st Royal Australian Regiment (1 RAR) took responsibility for the city of Baidoa, an inland city and the second largest in Somalia. Prior to the operation's deployment, the city had been a stronghold of the Somalia Liberation Army (SLA) – a group that wanted to assert itself as the major military power in the city. After assessing the environment, the commander of *Operation Solace* decided that he would position the force above the local warlords. This concept called for a show of strength on the part of the Australians, so as to 'ensure local respect'[25] for their presence. The operation prioritised security, practiced active disarmament and established 'domination of the HRS

[Humanitarian Relief Sector] through the use of static security positions, patrolling and on-call quick reaction forces'.[26]

The basis of the presence was a rule-of-law project intended to empower local clan leaders and restore local confidence; within a short period, rule of law had been jump-started (police and judiciary) and a local SLA criminal leader was subsequently arrested and convicted. A day later, the SLA fled Baidoa[27] and a local grassroots group, known as the SDM Baidoa, emerged as the 'major political force in the town'.[28] While deployed, *Operation Solace* took on 'total immersion', a style of 'community-orientated' peacekeeping, which was 'purposeful, low-tech, integrated and participatory'.[29] For the most part, 1 RAR operated under the tried-and-tested method of on-foot patrolling. This connected them to the community, and allowed them to tap into and make use of human intelligence.

Political–military interface

A UN force must seek to assert military power during the first phase of deployment, as well as in times of transition, and when new commanders are assigned to lead the force. Armed groups usually learn the limits of a UN force by probing for weaknesses at these key times. If UN forces cede the initiative to spoilers, then the mission will always be working to regain its lost deterrent value. Far too many past missions have failed to establish themselves as Chapter VII credible. As a result, future UN missions may struggle to project a credible deterrent factor, because they cannot trade on the UN's brand.

In complex multi-spoiler environments, UN forces should move to firmly tackle the strongest spoiler first. Such action should serve as a useful precedent and a warning to other or would-be spoilers. Mediators can leverage such offensives at a later time, to remind leaders of the risks of spoiler activity. As seen in the DRC, the use of the FIB against M23, and the eventual disbandment of the group brought numerous affiliated groups into the disarmament process. As this case indicates, robust peacekeeping cannot work unless it supports a genuine political process or a negotiated disarmament (DDR programme). The action of UN forces should always be seen as being intrinsically linked to the overall political or disarmament process, for which it serves. Indeed, the military actions of UN forces should nest within a coherent political strategy.

However, if a leader is to commit his group to a process, he needs to be convinced both that the process is genuine, and that it will actually serve his and the group's interests. To these ends, joining the political process must work as an incentive, so as to provide the most attractive non-violent alternative for spoilers seeking lower-cost alternatives to continued conflict. The political process should, therefore, be calibrated to embrace spoilers, while at the same time, not working to appease groups that enjoy limited popular support or serve narrow interest groups (such as business elites or warlords). As mentioned in Chapter Three, the placation of spoilers can work against longer-term sustainable peace by creating exclusive elite pacts or, worse, warlord governments.

Blowback and escalation

The use of force by peacekeepers can potentially draw the UN into an escalating confrontation with armed groups that have been targeted by robust action. There may also be blowback for civilians and other non-combatants. Thierry Tardy has argued that:

> Altering the nature of peace operations by adopting a more openly robust posture is likely to lead to some counter-reactions – in terms of host-country level of

acceptance, spoiler behaviour, impact on the local actors, or even TCC motives and behaviours that are difficult to predict. Robustness may deter some spoilers, but it may also induce reactions or new forms of disruption that would not have appeared otherwise.[30]

Armed groups subjected to robust peacekeeping have, in the past, displayed a tendency to learn from and adapt to each tactical engagement: they can atomise (break into smaller groups); dissolve into the civilian population; alter their tactics; and adopt enhanced asymmetrical postures. The application of force can also cause a split in armed groups, between military hardliners intent on continuing violence and those in the leadership cadre that prefer to pursue non-violent means of negotiation. Dealing with the adaptability of armed groups is a key consideration in the planning and conduct of operations. UN missions must try to anticipate likely changes in group structure, motivation and tactics, as well as a group's ability and willingness to escalate or retaliate. Planners must also take into account other armed groups in the picture, as these groups may seek to take advantage of the power vacuum created if robust operations weaken a targeted rival group.

The legitimate fear of many humanitarians is that groups subject to robust peacekeeping may retaliate against softer UN and NGO targets, as well as civilians, instead of risking re-engaging UN forces (i.e. hard targets). There are several reasons an armed group may do so. Firstly, spoilers can attack non-combatants or use hostages as a shield against robust UN action. Secondly, attacks on non-combatants can place considerable external pressure on a UN force and may result in the UN being forced to cease offensive operations. Thirdly, as the UN's focus on the protection of civilians is well known, spoilers might initiate a campaign of civilian victimisation with the intention of discrediting the mission in the eyes of both the international and local communities. Thus, soft-target retaliation by spoilers is designed to leverage the UN, with the eventual aim of forcing the mission to call off robust action.

UN missions cannot afford to be placed in such 'hostage and shield' positions, in which the utility of the mission is pinned to the whims of one or more of the parties. Otherwise, Machiavellian armed groups will seek to control a UN force and manipulate its actions to their ends.

The UN should also prepare against retaliatory attacks and plan for escalation. The key to robust peacekeeping, as previously mentioned, is the willingness to apply force in such a manner as to change a spoiler's behaviour. Robust operations should, therefore, be partly aimed at limiting a spoiler's natural inclination to retaliate. This may be challenging as the sting of a tactical defeat may evoke a strong urge for revenge among a group's leadership, especially if leaders are prone to irrational impulses. In order to guard against escalation, the UN must: establish itself as a superior force within its area of operation; employ a strong PPP concept; and undertake high-tempo operations of an unpredictable nature, designed to keep spoilers off balance. Finally, UN forces should anticipate likely sites of retaliation, and harden them against attack.

Constraints

The application of force in peacekeeping is subject to a range of constraints, and any discussion of robust peacekeeping should assume that the UN itself operates under resource limitations.[31] As UN forces are by their very nature multinational and each mission is different (in terms of composition and operating environment), the conduct of robust peacekeeping varies greatly; 'each UN mission will have its own parameters and constraints from which the mission commanders will have to determine if and how to apply force robustly.'[32] Constraints at the strategic, operational and tactical level include the following:

Mandate

It is often argued that military commanders need clarity, an unambiguous mandate on which to prosecute their action. Clarity, however, is decidedly lacking in most mandates, the problem being that 'all Security Council resolutions, without exception, reflect a measure of political compromise which in turn lends the mandate to differing interpretations. In some cases, the nature of that compromise has involved the commitment to an 'end state' so vague as to provide little or no basis for translation into realizable military objectives.'[33]

Rules of engagement (ROE)

Rules of engagement (ROE) provide the authority for the use of force and 'explain the legal framework, policies, principles, responsibilities and definitions' for each peacekeeping operation.[34] The restrictions applied by the ROE are not usually a problem in themselves, but rather the 'differences of opinion on the Rules of Engagement between contingents and the Mission' that may arise.[35]

Force generation

The units deployed by TCCs vary greatly in capacity and quality – a force can be a veritable assortment of light infantry, mechanised infantry, guard units and special forces. Certain units simply do not have the appropriate profile and capabilities required to conduct sustained robust peacekeeping. Composition, therefore, restricts the capacity of a force to deter spoilers, and, if need be, coerce them. During the force-generation process, it is often the case that the UN requests TCCs provide them with troops regardless of their capability or quality. While many missions have a mandated troop ceiling of 10,000–20,000 troops (such as UNAMID, UNMISS, MINUSMA, and MONUSCO), sheer numbers alone do not make for effective peacekeeping – the quality of those troops is equally important.[36]

Peacekeeping culture

The UN as an organisation has a culture that is adverse to the use of force: 'while recognized as sometimes necessary, [the use of force] is seen as anathema to the institution's broader pacific purpose.'[37] This aversion was clearly on display during the crisis in the Balkans, where there existed a 'pervasive ambivalence within the United Nations regarding the role of force in the pursuit of peace'.[38] The UN, as a whole, has slowly begun to realise that force beyond self-defence is a necessary component of peacekeeping. However, many actors – TCCs, SRSGs and certain member states – remain somewhat reluctant to fully embrace a Chapter VII mentality.

Troop contributing countries (TCCs)

Robust peacekeeping is constrained by the willingness of TCCs to risk their troops in the conduct of robust operations. While, on the one hand, robust operations involve greater risk, the major troop contributors are highly risk averse; many TCCs are unwilling to operate in the more dangerous environments. Although this risk aversion is entirely natural, it is arguably the single most limiting factor in the conduct of robust peace-keeping.

It is also clear that TCCs and the Security Council do not fully agree on the conduct of peacekeeping operations. Several major contributors have expressed their discomfort with robust peacekeeping, and have sought to downplay the use of force in their approaches; these include India, Uruguay, Bangladesh and Brazil. TCCs have 'made abundantly clear their disquiet with undertaking even robust peacekeeping'.[39] A shared understanding of robust peacekeeping among all TCCs would enable the respective UN force to make a unified effort. If TCCs are not 100% committed to the application of robust peacekeeping, then the Security Council has two choices: recruit a new set of contributors who are willing to expose their troops to the inherent risks of robust peacekeeping, or limit the ambitiousness of peacekeeping mandates to better reflect the inclinations of TCCs. Before this, however, it might be necessary to first articulate what robust peacekeeping actually means in practice. The Indian Permanent Representative recently complained that 'robust peacekeeping has not been properly defined'.[40]

National contingent commanders

In theory, the UN Force Commander exercises operational control over the entire UN force. However, in practice, 'nations deal directly with their contingents on the ground, [which sometimes confounds the force commander] who is attempting to employ them within his plan'.[41] Every time a force commander issues an order, the respective contingent commander must make a calculation: defer to his national headquarters, or follow the order issued by the force commander. A national contingent commander serves, at most, a couple of years with the UN, while his national military career might span 35 years. It is, therefore, usually an easy decision to make, unless the force commander can persuade the individual otherwise. This requires finesse on the part of the force commander, as well as strong ties with his brigade and sector commanders.[42]

Command and Control (C2)

Jean-Marie Guéhenno and Jake Sherman have argued that 'the UN model ... seems to combine the worse [sic] of two worlds:

too much military decentralization and too much political control over the conduct of military operations.'[43] Indeed, the UN grapples with many of the C2 maladies familiar to every multinational force – differences in languages, interoperability, training and military cultures. The job of the force commander is to engender cohesiveness, and combine all the disparate strands of the force together. UN missions, however, are formatted using a sector structure, with particular national contingents establishing themselves and operating in particular geographical areas. According to General Rupert Smith, former UN commander, this means that the force cannot be used effectively as a whole. Crucially, 'the willingness of UN leaders to act and react remains one of the major means for the UN to be effective. A mission can have the strongest mandate, robust ROE, well-trained troops and equipment, [but] if its commanders do not have the will or determination to take action, nothing much will happen.'[44]

Information

It is critical for peacekeepers to obtain as much information as possible about the objectives and motives of armed groups. Peacekeepers need to build 'an accurate picture of all armed groups, militias and criminal gangs present in the area of operation and study their particular politics and techniques of violence'.[45] However, the capacity to collect and analyse information – and produce high-quality intelligence – is not one of the UN's strong suits. It is, nevertheless, a key requirement of military activity and, therefore, robust peacekeeping. Military intelligence (G2) remains the domain of TCCs, and the mission remains dependent on the capacities of contingents. Although the UN has improved its capacity in information gathering through the Joint Mission Analysis Centre (JMAC) and the Joint Operations Centre (JOC), a considerable void remains in intelligence and analysis terms. The UN's web-like system is a potential gold mine for information, because it is a system that harnesses personnel – humanitarian workers, peacekeepers and civil-affairs officers – many of whom work across a wide region. The potential of the system, however, has yet to be fully realised, as the UN has not sought to develop a coherent, centralised arrangement to support the continuous flow of credible, timely and multi-source information.

In *Operation Khukri* in Sierra Leone (2000), the commanding general Lieutenant-General Jetley planned and executed the entire operation against the RUF rebels without knowledge of the location of the rebels' reserve force, the quantity of their weapons and ammunition, or the extent of their communications.[46] In a summary-of-action report, Jetley noted that UNAMSIL's 'ELINT [signals intelligence] and HUMINT [human intelligence] capabilities were non-existent'.[47] It so happened that the RUF were able to utilise their strong communications network to order their reserve forces into the fight; it was also later revealed that the rebels had considerable stores of 'warlike supplies'; both were details unknown to UNAMSIL.[48]

Logistical support and force enablers

Arguably, the most critical force enablers for robust peacekeeping are helicopters – utility, reconnaissance and attack. Helicopters enable mobility and mobility, in turn, allows peacekeepers to quickly traverse distance and terrain to achieve specific objectives. Despite their importance, UN missions continue to 'face a critical shortage of military helicopters'.[49] Attack helicopters have proven to be a key instrument in the conduct of robust operations (particularly in Côte d'Ivoire and the DRC). Attack helicopters offer several advantages, including greater precision targeting (using missiles and cannon), the element of surprise and firepower. In addition, they do not require forward observers and can be used for added deterrent value. During the FIB's campaign against M23, the use of South African Denel Rooivalk attack helicopters proved instrumental in defeating the group; three helicopters provided close-air support to ground units, and rocketed defensive positions and weapons caches.

As of 2011, the UN maintained 186 helicopters (including 12 attack helicopters) across all of its 16 missions. By comparison, in 2009, the US alone reportedly operated 120 helicopters of different varieties in Afghanistan.[50] Not only is the UN restricted by the numbers of helicopters but also by their usage: civilian helicopters make up the bulk of its air fleet (60%). These helicopters are leased from mostly Russian and Ukrainian private contractors and are subject to civil-aviation regulations, which restrict their operations (in terms of flying hours, night flying, all-weather capability, insurance and budgeting). In order to ensure mobility and effectiveness, UN peacekeepers must operate from remote forward-operating bases, which need to be resupplied by helicopter. Moreover, helicopters (both attack and utility) require adequate logistical support. If these capabilities are not forthcoming, then the capacity of UN forces to carry out robust peacekeeping will be seriously impeded.

It has been argued in this chapter that in non-permissive environments, robust peacekeeping is required to create the space for the political process to take root. Without Chapter VII robustness, peacekeepers cannot be proactive on the ground. UN missions that employ robust peacekeeping should be prepared to actively influence a spoiler's decision-making. By doing so, a UN mission can attach a cost to spoiler activity, whilst at the same time empowering the political and DDR processes that underpin each mission.

Undoubtedly, robust peacekeeping remains an enterprise fraught with complexities. In order to be effective its uses and limitations must be fully understood. UN missions, therefore, require politically savvy leaders, informed by knowledge of the local political map, who can judiciously decide when to use force and when to mediate.

Notes

1. Jim Terrie, 'The Use of Force in UN Peacekeeping: The Experience of MONUC', *African Security Review*, vol. 18, no. 1, 2009, p. 26.
2. 'Report of the Panel on United Nations Peace Operations', *Security Council [S/2000/809] and General Assembly [A/55/305]* (New York: United Nations, 2000), p. 54.
3. *Ibid.*
4. Terrie, 'The Use of Force in UN Peacekeeping, p. 28.
5. Rupert Smith, *The Utility of Force: The Art of War in the Modern World* (New York: Vintage Books, 2008), pp. 323–4.
6. See Marc Lacey, 'U.N. Forces Using Tougher Tactics to Secure Peace', *New York Times*, 23 May 2005, http://www.nytimes.com/2005/05/23/international/africa/23congo.html?pagewanted=all&_r=0.
7. UNSG S/4389/1960, p. 5.
8. 'Report of the Panel on United Nations Peace Operations', p. ix.
9. Terrie, 'The Use of Force in UN Peacekeeping', p. 32.
10. Mats Berdal, 'Lessons Not Learned: The Use of Force in Peace Operations in the 1990s', *International Peacekeeping*, vol. 7, no. 4, November 2007, p. 67.
11. David Richards, *Taking Command* (London: Headline Publishing Group, 2014).
12. William Durch and Madeline England, 'The Purposes of Peace Operations', in NYC Center for International Cooperation (ed.), *Robust Peacekeeping: The Politics of Force* (New York: NYC CIC, 2009), p. 46.
13. *Ibid.*
14. Samantha Power, *Chasing the Flame: Sergio Vieira De Mello and the Fight to Save the World* (New York: Penguin Press, 2008), p. 324.
15. Derek Boothby, 'The Application of Leverage in Eastern Slavonia', in Jean Krasmo, Bradd Hayes and Donald Daniel (eds), *Leveraging for Success in Peace Operations* (Westport, CT: Greenwood, 2003), p. 124.
16. Achim Wennmann, 'Grasping the Financing and Mobilization Cost of Armed Groups: A New Perspective on Conflict Dynamics', *Contemporary Security Policy*, vol. 30, no. 2, August 2009.
17. David Richards, *Taking Command*.
18. DPKO Best Practices Unit, *UN Protection of Civilians PDT Standards: Module 5: Prevention and Response to Conflict-Related Sexual Violence* (New York: United Nations, 2011), p. 28.
19. Peter E. Westenkirchner, *Applied Concept: The Military Information Operations Function within a Comprehensive and Effects-Based Approach* (Bonn: Bundeswehr, 2009), pp. 21–2.
20. DPKO Best Practices Unit, *UN Protection of Civilians PDT Standards: Module 5*, p. 28.

21 *Ibid.*, p. 22.

22 Pjer Šimunović, 'A Framework for Success: Contextual Factors in the UNTAES Operation in Eastern Slavonia', *International Peacekeeping*, vol. 6, no. 1, Spring 1999, p. 132.

23 Derek Boothby, 'The Application of Leverage in Eastern Slavonia', p. 124.

24 *Ibid.*

25 Robert Patman, 'Disarming Somalia: The Contrasting Fortunes of United States and Australian Peacekeepers during United Nations Intervention, 1992–1993', *African Affairs*, vol. 96, no. 385, October 1997, p. 522.

26 *Ibid.*, p. 521.

27 The SLA were shown to have weak roots, and only operated within the coercive end of the spectrum of competitive control (see Chapter One).

28 Patman, 'Disarming Somalia' p. 526.

29 *Ibid.*, p. 528.

30 Thierry Tardy, 'Robust Peacekeeping: A False Good Idea', in Cedric de Coning, Andreas Oien Stensland and Thierry Tardy (eds), *Beyond the 'New Horizon'* (Oslo: NUPI Publications, 2010), p. 74.

31 Richard Gowan and Benjamin Tortolani, 'Robust Peacekeeping and its Limitations', in NYC Center for International Cooperation (ed.), *Robust Peacekeeping: The Politics of Force* (New York: NYC CIC, 2009).

32 Terrie, 'The Use of Force in UN Peacekeeping', p. 32.

33 Berdal, 'Lessons Not Learned', p. 62.

34 'United Nations Infantry Field Manual Volume I', in *Department of Peacekeeping Operations and Department of Field Support* (New York: United Nations, 2012), p. 50.

35 See Patrick Cammaert, 'MONUC as a Case Study in Multidimensional Peacekeeping in Complex Emergencies', http://responsibilityto protect.org/favoritacammaert.pdf

36 *Ibid.*

37 Terrie, 'The Use of Force in UN Peacekeeping', p. 27.

38 Matthew Krain, 'International Intervention and the Severity of Genocides and Politicides', *International Studies Quarterly*, vol. 49, September 2005, p. 368, citing 'United Nations Report of the Secretary General Pursuant to General Assembly Resolution 53/35: The Fall of Srebrenica' A/54/549 (New York: United Nations, 1999), p. 111.

39 Donald Daniel, 'Contemporary Patterns in Peace Operations, 2000–2010', in Alex Bellamy and Paul Williams (eds), *Providing Peacekeepers* (Oxford: Oxford University Press, 2013), p. 40.

40 *Ibid.*, p. 228.

41 Rupert Smith, *The Utility of Force: The Art of War in the Modern World*, p. 316.

42 Interview with Major-General Adrian Foster.

43 See Jean-Marie Guéhenno and Jake Sherman, 'Command and Control Arrangements in United Nations Peacekeeping Operations', *International Forum for the Challenges of Peace Operations*, 9 November 2009, http://www.operationspaix.net/ DATA/DOCUMENT/4998~v~ Command_and_Control_Arrangements_in_United_Nations_Peacekeeping_Operations.pdf.

44 See Cammaert, 'MONUC as a Case Study in Multidimensional Peacekeeping in Complex Emergencies'.

45 Paul Williams, *Enhancing Civilian Protection in Peace Operations: Insights from Africa* (Washington DC: National Defense University Press, 2010), p. 39.

46 Vijay Jetley, 'Op Khukri – The United Nations Operation Fought in Sierra Leone Part II', United Service Institute of India, http://www.usiofindia.org/Article/Print/?pub=Journal&pubno=568&ano=388.

47 *Ibid.*, pp. 1–4.

48 *Ibid.*

49 Jake Sherman, Alischa Kugel and Andrew Sinclair, 'Overcoming Helicopter Force Generation Challenges for UN Peacekeeping Operations', *International Peacekeeping*, vol. 19, no. 1, February 2012, p. 77.

50 See Marie Jackson, 'Helicopters 'Are No Magic Wand', BBC News, 13 July 2009, http://news.bbc.co.uk/1/hi/uk/8148174.stm

CHAPTER FIVE

Prioritising the protection of civilians

Over the past ten years, many thousands of lives have been lost through conflict. The statistics are sobering. In Darfur, ongoing insecurity has cost approximately 461,520 lives,[1] while in the neighbouring Democratic Republic of the Congo (DRC) cascading humanitarian crises driven by insecurity have resulted in the deaths of some 5.4 million.[2] Statistics alone, however, cannot adequately capture the nature of the barbarity of these conflicts. Stories of widespread mass rape of women, forced recruitment of child soldiers, and mass atrocity crimes continue to unfold.

In response to mass crimes and civilian victimisation, peace-keepers have in recent years been assigned the challenging task of protecting civilians. Brahimi's report outlined a set of expectations concerning the role of peacekeepers in the protection of civilians (POC):

> Indeed, peacekeepers – troops or police – who witness violence against civilians should be presumed to be authorized to stop it, within their means, in support of basic United Nations principles and, as stated in

the report of the Independent Inquiry on Rwanda, consistent with 'the perception and the expectation of protection created by [an operation's] very presence.[3]

Despite a difficult transition from a nascent concept to an essential mission task – marked by several calamitous protection failures that 'almost destroyed the UN itself'[4] – UN peacekeeping is now firmly wedded to the concept of POC.[5] The credibility of the enterprise is today prefaced on the notion that missions seek to actively protect civilians. There is a clear expectation, on the part of both international and local communities, that if peacekeepers are present in conflict situations they will protect civilians, and if they are not immediately present, that they will respond rapidly to protect. While the primary responsibility for POC rests with the host state, it is expected that peacekeepers will carry out POC when governments are unable or unwilling to provide such protection. This is a reasonably fair expectation. Still, UN peacekeeping missions are often seen as impotent witnesses to violence directed at civilian populations. Obviously, missions cannot protect everyone, everywhere, at all times. Nevertheless, if the mission is not seen to be doing its utmost to protect civilians then it will cease to hold the trust of the local population; MONUSCO, for instance, was at one time known as 'MON-useless' by many Congolese.[6] In non-permissive environments, armed groups emerge as the principal agents of victimisation and, therefore, the focus of UN POC efforts. To be effective, however, UN missions must first understand the motivations behind the perpetrators of violence.

Why do armed groups victimise civilians?

It would seem contradictory for an armed group to attack the very civilians it may rely on for future political, economic or social support. An armed group's reasons depend on its overall motivations and objectives – which can be altered to suit changes in circumstance, and as new opportunities arise.

Ethnic cleansing and genocide

At the extremities of civilian victimisation are genocide and ethnic cleansing. These are 'ends-based strategies of violence' where the objective of the armed group can only be achieved by attacking civilians as an end in itself.[7] Generally, mass killing on the scale of genocide is conceived of 'by a relatively small number of powerful political or military leaders acting in the service of their own interests, ideas, hatreds, fears'.[8] Political elites typically promote genocidal discrimination through 'propaganda and indoctrination'.[9] Ethnic cleansing has a slightly different emphasis: to expel an undesirable population from a particular territory for reasons of discrimination based on ethnic, religious, political or other criteria. While modern ethnic cleansing is pursued with a decidedly ideological fervour, pre-twentieth-century acts were generally utilitarian in nature – ethnic cleansing carried out for 'pursuing land, economic wealth, slaves, or simply settling old scores'.[10]

Retaliation and retribution

Perpetrators of violence might be motivated by revenge for past atrocities or immediate events. It is common for retaliation to take on a cyclical dimension, with reprisal and counter- reprisal. For example, at the beginning of the Lebanese civil war, unidentified gunmen fired on a church in the Ain el-Rummaneh district, killing four including two members of the Phalange Party. Only hours later, the Phalangists retaliated by massacring 30 Palestinians travelling on a bus through the neighbourhood. This type of violence is characteristic of many civil wars, as victim becomes perpetrator, and perpetrator becomes victim.

Brutalisation

Once political order breaks down, violence begets violence as fighters and civilians alike become exposed to the brutality of conflict. A culture of lawlessness creates a new norm of what is permissible. Under such conditions, it is common to hear of ill-disciplined fighters marauding across the countryside, extracting rent and brutalising the population. Sexual violence also forms a part of this conflict landscape. Rape is permitted and even encouraged in many settings for a variety of reasons. Commanders may want to 'boost morale' or 'reward' fighters for service. In many war zones, mass rape is used with a more strategic intention: to redraw the ethnic map (in Bosnia), or to humiliate the enemy and terrorise local communities (in Darfur), for example.

Capacities

In an analysis of insurgents challenging state forces for control of government or territory, Reed Wood argues that 'increasing rebel strength is positively related to lower levels of violence', essentially due to the fact that stronger groups 'are better equipped to make competitive offers to potential supporters. Comparatively capable insurgent groups, there-fore, have fewer incentives to resort to violence to acquire support.'[11] By contrast, weak armed groups facing resource-mobilisation problems engage in violence against civilians as a means to acquire necessary resources and prevent collab-oration with government forces or rival groups.[12] Under such circumstances, belligerents may victimise civilians to compensate for their decline in relative power and to deter rising threats. When civilians support the group, the incentive for violence is generally low; as resistance (or apathy) increases, armed groups are more willing to use violence.

Selective violence and the enforcement of order

Armed groups can use violence in a more selective fashion, to eliminate those civilians who have defected or continue to collaborate with an enemy. In these cases, 'means-based strategies of violence' are applied, where violence is the means to a different end and not the final objective.[13] Armed groups may attack civilians for cooperating or collaborating with their enemies,[14] or they may wish to control populations to deter them from supporting the government, punishing any person who does not conform to the rules of the system. Victimisation is thus more likely in areas in which support for the adversary is high or where the group suspects disloyalty.

Bargaining and imposing costs

According to Lisa Hultman, violence against civilians by armed groups is a strategy and not a consequence of war. It is 'strategic behaviour aimed to affect the balance of the rebels' relative bargaining power'.[15] Armed groups target civilians when they expect it might increase their chances of obtaining concessions from the government. If they believe the government is dependent on the support of the population, successful attacks against civilians may turn the population against a government unable to protect them. This is often a strategic calculation to obtain a better position for the armed group vis-à-vis the government, but will not necessarily endear the population to the group's cause. Armed groups may target civilians when they are unable to impose enough costs through direct battle, in order to at least damage the government's reputation.[16]

Countering civilian victimisation

Understanding the motivation behind an armed group's tactics can help determine appropriate strategies for countering them. Whether peacekeepers use force depends largely on how their commanders interpret their mandate. There are a number of practical questions force commanders face; which civilians should be protected? What is the area of protection? What means can peacekeepers use to protect? Should they use force or other means? If they do use force, how much can they use? Protecting 'civilians under imminent threat of physical violence' is not, therefore, as clear, on an operational or tactical level, as it might initially appear in the Security Council protection mandate.

Political engagement

The best protection is peace, and peace can be assured through political solutions. As shown in Chapter Three, UN missions can undertake mediation to engage armed groups with the aim of co-opting them into a political process. The same tract can be utilised as a POC tool. Political engagement aimed at protection, of course, need not be distinct from that which aims to bring about a cessation of general hostilities. The renunciation of violence might even be used as a precondition for inclusion in the political process. As outlined above, there are myriad drivers of victimisation: 'identity factors, perceived historical wrongs, territorial claims, racism bred out of fear, desire to extend political control or impose a political ideology, economic issues, support for criminal enterprises, or establishment of a reign by terror'.[17] Political engagement must be tailored to address and ultimately eliminate these different drivers.

In the current climate of peacekeeping, political engagement constitutes a central strategy, considering the reluctance of TCCs and missions to draw on the use of force to protect civilians. In the report of the Office of Internal Oversight Services (OIOS) on the protection of civilians, several TCCs emphasised the political tract over the use of force: '... political robustness [was seen by TCCs as a better way] of protecting people than "buying tanks for peacekeepers" and the use of force was justified only for the self-defence of peacekeepers themselves'.[18] Yet, political engagement can be unduly prolonged, or even ultimately futile, while in the meantime civilian victimisation continues. Civilians in dire need of protection cannot always rely on the promise of a future agreement or the dead-letter assurances of perpetrators. They require the tangible protection afforded by military peacekeepers.

Prevention

The objective of prevention is simple: to stop civilian victimisation or mass-atrocity crimes from occurring. Judgements about the effectiveness of preventative deployments are, nevertheless, fraught. This is because for preventative action to be judged effective, in simple terms, nothing happens (there is no massacre). Moreover, prevention requires a strong capacity to predict the course of civilian-victimisation events. However, as Paul Williams suggests, 'the problem, of course, is that it is very difficult for peacekeepers to predict where massacres might occur or to stop those taking place outside their areas of deployment.'[19] In order to anticipate mass killing, Benjamin Valentino argues that 'we must begin to think of it [mass killing] in the same way perpetrators do'.[20]

In 1994, the UN failed to prevent, and then adequately respond to, the Rwandan genocide. A modest UN force, UNAMIR, was deployed to the country, in late 1993, to oversee the implementation of the Arusha Accords, which had been signed between the Hutu-led government and the Tutsi-led Rwandan Patriotic Front (RPF). In the lead-up to the genocide, many Hutu became radicalised under the Hutu Power ideology. Hutu Power groups also began to arm themselves in preparation for large-scale violence (to kill 1,000 people an hour). The UN Secretariat, however, failed to give Lieutenant-General Romeo Dallaire, UNAMIR's force commander, the authorisation to act *pre-emptively* to disrupt the activities of the would-be génocidaires – the militias of the Impuzamugambi and the Interahamwe. The Independent Inquiry on Rwanda found that, although UNAMIR had no explicit mandate to protect civilians, it was expected that the peacekeeping operation would respond in the event of mass-atrocity crimes.

The lessons of Rwanda suggest that prevention may require responding decisively to the early-warning signs of ends-based violence (such as genocide and ethnic cleansing). This might involve UN forces destroying weapons caches or training camps,[21] striking the C2 centres of gravity, and dismantling the means to broadcast hate speech (as with Radio Télévision Libre des Mille Collines in Rwanda). The key to preventing ends-based violence is to break inertia and act quickly, because inaction 'contributes most to situations of genocide and mass atrocities'.[22] The UN must also consider pre-empting, through deterrence, retaliatory violence, which if left unchecked can escalate a situation rapidly. Populations under immediate threat might also need to be evacuated to a safer location, if the UN, the host government or a local militia cannot ensure security at their location. Such a policy can amount to ethnic cleansing, but sometimes difficult decisions of this kind need to be made. The evacuation of Muslim communities from Bangui in CAR to safer regions near the Chadian border was necessary due to a complete lack of security in the capital.

A key component of prevention is deterrence: being in the right place at the right time and presenting the right posture. Peacekeepers can 'deter violence through military presence',[23] but a higher level of deterrence can only be achieved by demonstrating a robust posture; the 'willingness to use force against belligerents'[24] acts to discourage attacks on civilians. The UK's

Operation Palliser in Sierra Leone is an example of a force that was able to establish credibility by demonstrating its capabilities. UN missions can also deter potential perpetrators through the 'power of witness': the willingness to expose the actions of a perpetrator group to international and local scrutiny with the aim of motivating it to behave responsibly.[25]

Interposition

An interpositional strategy involves the insertion of peacekeepers between the perpetrators of violence and the victims (or potential victims). The Mass Atrocity Response Operation (MARO) project proposes six military approaches to civilian protection, two of which conform to the concept of interposition, those being separation and safe zones. At its heart, interposition is a defensive strategy, which pursues the goal of physically protecting civilians under threat of violence, rather than directly confronting the perpetrators of violence. When civilians fear for their lives, many naturally flee to UN bases with the expectation of protection. For instance, in Bunia, DRC, prior to the deployment of EUFOR Artemis in 2003, a large number of civilians fled advancing local militia and sought shelter around the perimeter of the UN base. Likewise, during the ongoing conflict in South Sudan, UNMISS bases were opened to accommodate large numbers of civilians.

The creation of safe areas allows peacekeepers to focus their efforts around highly concentrated areas of vulnerable populations, such as internally displaced persons (IDP) camps or UN bases. Peacekeepers provide security for civilians through the removal of 'threats from direct and indirect fires'[26] within the safe area and its surroundings – with zones beyond the safe area being regularly patrolled and monitored.[27] Safe areas need to be completely demilitarised to ensure that armed combatants are not allowed to operate among the protected civilian population. Protection can also be achieved with fewer forces, which suits the UN's inherent limitations. However, as the events of Srebrenica highlighted, safe areas can only be made safe when UN forces are willing to repel attacks. In practice, there is a danger that perpetrator groups may bide their time while preparing to overwhelm UN forces through a decisive attack on protected populations.

Safe areas also create de facto unsafe areas – regions where peacekeepers have ceded the initiative to perpetrators. Such a scenario may speed up the occurrence of ethnic cleansing and 'legitimize long-term refugee/IDP relocation'.[28]

Filling the security vacuum

As academic Simon Chesterman has rightly suggested, 'the single most important aim of any peace operation is to establish the conditions for sustainable security for the civilian population'.[29] Hard security is paramount to ensuring political stability, and therefore the long-term viability of the mission itself, and the state as a whole. Governance, development and security are mutually reinforcing – with security being the bedrock upon which the other two are founded. Creating conditions for security can, nevertheless, be incredibly challenging as peacekeepers are always deployed slowly and in limited numbers (usually 10,000–20,000 troops).

Filling the security vacuum is particularly important in countries such as CAR, where attacks against Muslim communities have been carried out under a blanket of impunity. UN High Commissioner for Human Rights Navi Pillay has highlighted the security-gap problem well: 'people apprehended with blood on their machetes and severed body parts in their hands have been allowed to go free because there is nowhere to detain them and no means to charge them with the crimes they have clearly committed.'[30] In these fragile security situations, the use of Formed Police Units (FPUs) might be useful in dealing 'with riots and other conflicts prevailing among a civilian population such as rampant lawlessness, revenge killings, and major civil disturbances aimed at derailing a peace process'.[31] A host of other law-and-order mechanisms are required to support FPUs, including mobile courts and interim detention facilities. Quickly re-establishing sanctioning mechanisms (that is, the rule of law) can also be effective by raising the costs of violent activity.

The use of force

The notion that force should be used to bring an end to civilian victimisation – through robust peacekeeping – operates under the logic that it is easier to take on the perpetrators of violence than to undertake interposition activities (safe zones or separation) to protect the victims of violence.[32] Despite the evidence to suggest that 'campaigns to defeat the perpetrators had a better success rate than those to save the victims, probably because those who intervened tended to underestimate the demands involved in the "easier" option', TCCs remain reluctant to use force in this way.[33] Moreover, a recent OIOS report noted that some missions, namely UNAMID and UNMISS, felt 'weak, outnumbered and stretched across vast areas, making the use of force only a paper option'.[34]

The military needs to consider how its approach may alter the level and dynamics of attacks against civilians. For example, when armed groups are intent on the violent control of civilian populations, attempts to dislodge them by force may increase the subsequent level of violence against civilians in the form of reprisals.[35] The LRA 'almost systematically retaliates against civilians in response to military attacks. The regional armies and the peacekeeping missions alike have disclaimed responsibility for failing to protect civilians.'[36] In 2009, MONUC's support of efforts by the DRC's national army to disarm one armed group led to massive retaliation against civilians. Therefore, peacekeeping operations not only need information about the motivations and objectives, but also the capabilities of the armed groups they face, and a sober assessment of the potential impact the use of coercive force may have on the very civilians the peacekeepers aim to protect.

Conceptual challenges

One challenge UN missions face with protection mandates is the perception that responsibility for protection lies with the peacekeepers. This is often the impression and expectation of the media and local population and when such expectations are not met, the credibility of the mission and the UN as a whole is brought into question. This perception can incorrectly shift the blame away from the groups targeting civilians. It can also reinforce the erroneous notion that peacekeepers, rather than host governments, have the primary responsibility to protect civilians. Protection of civilians is unequivocally a national responsibility. When the state is unwilling or incapable of protecting its citizens from violent actions by armed groups, or when the state's security forces are responsible for some of the violence being perpetrated against its own civilians, then the situation becomes even more complex for the peacekeeping mission. It is imperative that the objective of the UN mission is made clear, not only to the peacekeepers and other UN personnel, but also to the host government, media and local population.

Another challenge is the fact that, even though 15 years have passed since Resolution 1265 (declaring the role of the Security Council in conflict prevention), there is still no clear and unified definition of what protection of civilians entails within the UN system.[37] This makes it difficult for peacekeepers to know who exactly they are meant to protect and what type of protection they need to provide. Protection of civilians can be distinguished into three broad categories: physical, legal and humanitarian. Political action is required to address the causes of conflict; military action, to address its symptoms; and humanitarian action, to address its effects.[38]

The numerous humanitarian agencies and other international organisations on the ground, of course, each have a different agenda and different interpretation of protection. For example, humanitarian agencies may consider protection as the fulfilment of human rights and legal norms under international humanitarian law, whereas to military institutions, it would most likely mean the physical defence of civilians or installations, demilitarisation of 'safe areas', and so on.[39] This lack of common understanding about what protection means makes the groundwork for operations and division of responsibilities between military, humanitarian and other actors inherently difficult.[40]

Another reason why there may still be no agreement on how to achieve POC is that some Security Council members may fear a clear definition will prove binding or undermine state sovereignty and territorial integrity.[41] In a report on six decades of UN peacekeeping operations, Victoria Holt and Glyn Taylor concluded that:

> No (Security) Council document offers an operational definition of what protection of civilians means for peacekeeping missions, nor has the Council tasked the Secretariat, which may be the most appropriate organ to develop such guidelines, to do so.[42]

This uncertainty is a central obstacle to rendering POC effective in UN peace operations.[43] Further, the report suggests that mandates are mere political statements and negotiated texts, which are meant to give direction to peacekeepers, rather than operational documents that lay out the specifics of the mission and the modes of action to take.[44]

As a result, DPKO has sought to articulate POC for peace-keepers as a multidimensional concept, encompassing the full range of physical, political and human-rights activities.[45] The Draft Operational Concept of Protection of Civilians and United Nations Peacekeeping Operations (2010) (Capstone) organises POC into three tiers of engagement: protection through the political process; protection from physical violence; and the establishment of a protective environment.[46] DPKO is at the forefront of developing policies, doctrines, strategies, concepts, planning tools and training modules to advance the organisa-tion's capability to protect civilians in armed conflict. Still, none of these have a consistent or unified definition of what POC entails.[47] This has led to peacekeeping troops improvising in the field.[48] From a military perspective, protection mandates are qualitatively different from traditional peacekeeping operations.[49] Therefore, not only is there a need to clarify the exact expectations of protection mandates from a political and strategic perspective, but attention also needs to be given to the approaches typically taken by military organisations and how these can be integrated with the political objectives of the mandate.

Operational issues

Peacekeeping missions are notoriously under-resourced, which can hamper their ability to protect civilians effectively, particu-larly in areas where the force is spread thinly over wide and challenging terrain. Modern-day missions are being conducted 'in some of the most insecure and logistically challenging parts of the world, while mandated to carry out multiple tasks apart from civilian protection'.[50] At the same time, they are 'facing enormous resource constraints and consequently have difficulty fulfilling their mandate.'[51] In the DRC, POC is only one of 40 other tasks of MONUSCO;[52] so clearly trade-offs between different tasks must be considered. According to Security Council Resolution 1894, mandated protection activities must be given priority in making decisions about the use of resources.[53] With peacekeepers responsible for protecting civilians, their own personal security and that of other UN personnel and assets, adequate resources are, therefore, essential to ensure troops are given the best possible chance to effectively carry out their mandated tasks.

Initial resources allocated to peacekeeping missions may be insufficient, particularly if the force was initially configured to keep the peace, but the peace does not subsequently hold and there are increased attacks against civilians. Paul Williams notes that, as a rule of thumb, there should be between two and ten troops per 1,000 civilians in a crisis zone, or that the protection force should be at least the same size as the largest indigenous force.[54] Using the example of the DRC (MONUSCO) and Sudan (UNMIS/UNMISS), Williams demonstrates the gross under-resourcing for both of these missions.[55] The other issue is that deployment is often slow and generally reactive to crises on the ground, with troop numbers increasing only after crises erupt. In addition to military troops, police troops are often required, particularly if a country lacks the rule of law and it needs to be enforced at a local level.[56]

Other resource challenges peacekeeping operations face include: insufficient numbers of specialised units, such as engineers, medics, intelligence gatherers, special forces and interpreters; not having the correct type and number of vehicles, such as helicopters, armoured personnel carriers and unmanned aerial vehicles; and having inadequate communications and logistical support.[57]

At times, the sheer logistical challenge of protecting civilians against violence perpetuated over massive territories, in harsh terrain, and with little or poor infrastructure, like in the DRC and Sudan, can make it 'virtually impossible for any operation to have the size, equipment, mobility, funding and coordination capacity to effectively protect the millions of civilians that are being threatened'.[58] Armed groups using guerrilla warfare know their terrain and environment, so even the most robust mission may find it difficult to protect civilians scattered throughout such territory. The operational environment can clearly be complex. Some missions face large numbers of armed groups and, even if one group is suppressed, another may quickly arise in its place. Thus, even as peacekeepers work to contain and control armed groups, it is essential that political processes are made to work in tandem with military operations to bring an end to the conflict.

Peacekeepers must also make decisions on which civilians require urgent protection, and which cannot be protected for lack of capacity. Physical-protection mandates that require civilians under 'imminent threat' to be protected are interpreted differently by different missions. The 2014 OIOS report identified a number of central dilemmas that confronted peacekeepers, and 'gaps at the tactical level on the issue of how to respond to complex and ambiguous situations that might require the use of force'.[59] In the report, many peacekeepers made it clear that they remained unsure as to what they should do when: fighting occurred between two or more armed groups; armed groups were embedded among the population; the imminence of threat could not be evaluated; they were outnumbered; they could not rely on the availability of reinforcements; or it was difficult to access the site of civilian victimisation.

More work, in the form of policy, guidance, pre-deployment and scenario training, needs to be done to ensure that peacekeepers can better deal with such situations. Better guidance should come not only from the Office of Military Affairs (OMA)/DPKO, but also from each individual TCC.

Information gap

It is critical for peacekeepers to obtain as much information about the objectives and motives of armed groups as possible in order to adequately protect civilians. However, most missions do not have sufficient intelligence-gathering capacity. Peacekeepers need to build 'an accurate picture of all armed groups, militias and criminal gangs present in the area of operation and study their particular politics and techniques of violence'.[60] For example, analysts have identified that in the DRC there are nearly 20 armed factions; mapping threats and identifying perpetrators is therefore crucial for effective planning.[61] It is also important to understand the expectations of local populations and what they need by way of protection. Ignoring local perceptions and priorities in this respect has been described as the 'most common failure [of UN missions]'.[62] Missions, therefore, need to monitor local media and be aware of the bigger picture.

Information can be gathered from peaceful locals, as well as from local resistance groups. Strong relations with populations are not only important for information gathering, but also for implementing early-warning capacity building and trust. Yet, some locals may be ambivalent or even hostile towards a peacekeeping intervention,[63] and in such circumstances other strategies need to be employed. MONUC has addressed this with the establishment of Joint Protection Teams (JPTs), which are 'small ad hoc teams of UN civilian, military and police staff with diverse expertise that deploy to high-risk areas to generate recommendations for advancing protection of civilians and building confidence between the UN and local communities'.[64]

One benefit of these teams has been the increased 'situational awareness across the mission through timely, corroborated updates from otherwise inaccessible areas'.[65] A drawback is the fact that they are formed in response to emergencies and so, while being able to investigate and assess protection risks where attacks are rumoured to occur, they are reactive rather than proactive in terms of information gathering. Also, JPTs are typically only in the field for up to one week, so their ability to gain the trust of locals and provide long-term benefits to missions is limited.

Peacekeeping operations require the ability to systematically collect and analyse information to assess threats from armed groups, and then to determine the kinds of protection to be offered and from where it should come.[66] JPTs help provide some of this information. Other useful sources include non-governmental, humanitarian and international organisations situated on the ground, with access to the local population and sometimes even to armed groups. At the same time, humanitarian agencies have different perspectives on what constitutes 'protection', often leading to tension and confusion over competing objectives. In 2005, the Inter Agency Standing Committee (IASC) attempted to address this issue by devising an integrated approach to protection, whereby UN entities with humanitarian responsibilities and other international actors would establish protection clusters to address gaps, provide leadership resources and improve coordination amongst the various agencies. These protection clusters are now overseen by the Global Protection Cluster in all those countries with protection mandates.[67]

One of the main sources of tension between UN missions and humanitarian agencies is that many humanitarian agencies see any coordination with peacekeepers as compromising their appearance of neutrality. As these agencies need to deal with all actors in a conflict, including armed groups, their impartiality is crucial. However, with more civilians (and humanitarian personnel) being targeted by armed groups, the question of protection is increasingly one of how far this responsibility extends and how to include it in an integrated peacekeeping operation, rather than whether there will be integration at all.[68] Moreover, as Paul Bonard, ICRC ex-deputy director for protection, points out, 'if the mandate of peacekeeping forces is truly neutral and aimed at the protection of civilians, humanitarian players should support it and cooperate with the troops on the ground in order to protect civilians'.[69] In the DRC, MONUC and UNHCR have cooperated on protection, but the same cannot be said of all missions and this gap needs to be addressed.

Political support from the host government is imperative to the success of a peacekeeping operation with a protection mandate. Such support helps with: physically protecting civilians; continually engaging the parties to the conflict; bringing armed groups to the negotiating table; and sanctioning them when they violate citizens' fundamental rights.[70] There is, however, no systematic link between Security Council protection mandates and political strategies to achieve these objectives.[71] Even when sanctions have been imposed on armed groups, for example, they have been 'consistently violated but the Security Council takes no further steps to counter this'.[72] Often, host governments are not in a position to protect civilians and may even be involved in attacks against civilians. The dual-edged sword of needing the host government's consent to have a peacekeeping force in the country, with the knowledge that such consent can be withdrawn at any time, is a further 'weak link' in the protection chain.[73]

Peacekeepers face numerous challenges in their mandates to protect civilians from armed groups. The DPKO has attempted to fill some of these operational gaps and the willingness of the Security Council to use more robust forces in certain situations appears to indicate that deficiencies are being addressed, albeit slowly and in a reactive manner. Without a systematic approach, however, UN missions will continue to face difficulties as they try to fulfil protection mandates.

Notes

1   Olivier Degomme and Debarati Guha-Sapir, 'Patterns of Mortality Rates in Darfur Conflict', *Lancet*, vol. 375, no. 9711, January 2010.

2   International Rescue Committee and the Burnet Institute, *Mortality in the Democratic Republic of Congo: An Ongoing Crisis* (New York: IRC, 2007), p. 16.

3   Report of the Panel on United Nations Peace Operations, A/55/305 (New York: United Nations, 2000), p. 11.

4   Interview with Jean-Marie Guéhenno, in *Mandated to Protect: Protection of Civilians in Peace Operations* (Geneva: UNITAR, 2011).

5   Victoria Holt and Glyn Taylor, *Protecting Civilians in the Context of UN Peacekeeping Operations: Successes, Setbacks and Remaining Challenges* (Advance Copy), (New York: DPKO and OHCA, 2009).

6   See Gabriel Gatehouse, 'DR Congo: UN's Failed Illusion of Security in the East', BBC News, 24 May 2013, http://www.bbc.co.uk/news/world-africa-22659342.

7   Alexander Beadle, *Finding the 'Utility of Force to Protect' – Towards a Theory of Protection of Civilians – Rapport 2011/01889* (Kjeller: Norwegian Defence Research Establishment, 2011), p. 19.

8   Benjamin A. Valentino, *Final Solutions: Mass Killing and Genocide in the 20th Century* (Ithaca and London: Cornell University Press, 2013).

9   *Ibid*.

10   Derek Davis, 'Confronting Ethnic Cleansing in the Twenty-first Century', *Journal of Church and State*, vol. 42, no. 4, 2000, p. 695.

11   Reed Wood, 'Rebel Capability and Strategic Violence against Civilians,' *Journal of Peace Research*, vol. 47, no. 5, 2010, p. 612.

12   *Ibid*.

13   Beadle, *Finding the 'Utility of Force to Protect'*, p. 24.

14   *Ibid*., p. 19.

15   Lisa Hultman, *Targeting the Unarmed: Strategic Rebel Violence in War* (Uppsala: Uppsala University, Department of Peace and Conflict Research, 2008), p. 14.

16   *Ibid*., pp. 14–15.

17   Sarah Sewall, Dwight Raymond, and Sally Chin, *Mass Atrocity Response Operations: A Military Planning Handbook* (Cambridge: Harvard Kennedy School and PKSOI, 2010), p. 45.

18   'Evaluation of the Implementation and Results of Protection of Civilians Mandates in United Nations Peacekeeping Operations', A/68/787 (New York: United Nations, 2014), p. 13.

19   Paul Williams, *Enhancing Civilian Protection in Peace Operations:*

Insights from Africa – Africa Center for Strategic Studies Research Paper No. 1 (Washington DC: National Defense University, 2010), p. 38.

20 Benjamin A. Valentino, *Final Solutions.*

21 See Romeo Dallaire, *Shake Hands with the Devil: The Failure of Humanity in Rwanda* (Cambridge, MA: Da Capo, 2003), pp. 142–8.

22 Clint Hinote, *Campaigning to Protect: Using Military Force to Stop Genocide and Mass Atrocities* (Cambridge, MA: MARO Project, 2008), p. 33.

23 Sewall, Raymond and Chin, *Mass Atrocity Response Operations*, p. 99.

24 Victoria Holt and Joshua Smith, *Halting Widespread or Systematic Attacks on Civilians: Military Strategies and Operational Concepts – a Workshop Report* (Washington DC: The Henry L. Stimson Center, 2008), p. 22.

25 Sarah Sewall, Dwight Raymond, and Sally Chin, *Mass Atrocity Response Operations*, p. 69.

26 *Ibid.*, p. 78.

27 *Ibid.*, pp. 77–8.

28 *Ibid.*, p. 78.

29 Simon Chesterman, *External Study: The Use of Force in UN Peace Operations* (New York: DPKO Peacekeeping Best Practices Unit, 2004), p. 12.

30 See Serge Leger Kokpakpa, 'U.N. Official Says "Terrifying" Level of Hatred in Central African Republic', Reuters, 20 March 2014, http://uk.reuters.com/article/2014/03/20/uk-centralafrica-un-idUKBREA2J1RY20140320.

31 Benjamin Kwasi Agordzo, 'Filling the "Security Gap" in Post-conflict Situations: Could Formed Police Units Make a Difference?', *International Peacekeeping*, vol. 16, no. 2, April 2009, p. 288.

32 Williams, *Enhancing Civilian Protection in Peace Operations*, pp. 48–9.

33 *Ibid.*, p. 57.

34 'Evaluation of the Implementation and Results of Protection of Civilians Mandates in United Nations Peacekeeping Operations', p. 15.

35 Daniel Levine, 'Civilian Protection and the Image of the "Total Spoiler": Reflections on MONUC Support in Kimia II', *African Security Review*, vol. 20, no. 1, March 2011.

36 Héloïse Ruaudel, '"Catch me if you can!" The Lord's Resistance Army', *Forced Migration Review*, vol. 37, March 2011, p. 14.

37 Stian Kjeksrud, Jacob Aasland Ravndal, Andreas Øien Stensland, Cedric de Coning, Walter Lotze and Erin A. Weir, *Protection of Civilians in Armed Conflict – Comparing Organisational Approaches*, rapport 2011/01888 (Kjeller: Norwegian Defence Research Establishment: Norwegian Defence Research Establishment, 2011), p.12.

38 Marta Martinelli, *The Protection of Civilians during Peacekeeping Operations* (Brussels: European Parliament, 2008), p. 11.

39 Williams, *Enhancing Civilian Protection in Peace Operations*, p. 21.

40 Maritinelli, *The Protection of Civilians during Peacekeeping Operations*, pp. 9–10.

41 Security Council Report, *Cross-Cutting Report: The Protection of Civilians* (New York: Security Council Report, October 2008), p. 28.

42 Victoria Holt and Glyn Taylor, *Protecting Civilians in the Context of UN Peacekeeping Operations: Successes, Setbacks and Remaining Challenges*

(Advance Copy), (New York: DPKO and OHCA, 2009), p. 57.

43 *Ibid.*

44 *Ibid*, p. 76.

45 Stian Kjeksrud et al., *Protection of Civilians in Armed Conflict*, p. 22.

46 *Ibid.*, p. 23, citing 'DPKO/DFS United Nations Peacekeeping Operations Principles and Guidelines' (New York: United Nations, 2008), p. 24.

47 Stian Kjeksrud et al., *Protection of Civilians in Armed Conflict*, p. 23.

48 Julie Reynaert, *MONUC/MONUSCO and Civilian Protection in the Kivus* (Antwerp: International Peace Information Service, 2011), p. 8.

49 Stian Kjeksrud et al., *Protection of Civilians in Armed Conflict*, p. 7.

50 Reynaert, *MONUC/MONUSCO and Civilian Protection in the Kivus*, p. 8.

51 *Ibid.*

52 *Ibid.*

53 'Resolution 1894', *UN Security Council* (reference no: S/RES/1894/2009), clause 19.

54 Michael O'Hanlon and Peter W. Singer, 'The Humanitarian Transformation: Expanding Global Intervention Capacity', *Survival*, vol. 46, no. 1, 2004.

55 Williams, *Enhancing Civilian Protection in Peace Operations*, pp. 27–8. According to this rule of thumb, as at 2008 in North Kivu, DRC, method one would require between 10,000–50,000 troops and method two approximately 20,000, whereas the actual number of peacekeeping troops on the ground numbered 6,000.

56 Security Council Report, *Protection of Civilians: Cross Cutting Report: No. 2*, p. 24.

57 Williams, *Enhancing Civilian Protection in Peace Operations*, p. 28.

58 Martinelli, *The Protection of Civilians during Peacekeeping Operations*, p. 10.

59 'Evaluation of the Implementation and Results of Protection of Civilians Mandates in United Nations Peacekeeping Operations.

60 Williams, *Enhancing Civilian Protection in Peace Operations*, p. 39.

61 *Ibid.*

62 See 'Protecting Civilians in Armed Conflict', note by director, The Ditchley Foundation, May 2013, http://www.ditchley.co.uk/conferences/past-programme/2010-2019/2013/protecting-civilians.

63 Martinelli, *The Protection of Civilians During Peacekeeping Operations*, p. 10.

64 Tobie Whitman, *Joint Protection Teams: A Model for Enhancing Civilian Security* (The Institute for Inclusive Security, Washington DC, November 2010), p.1.

65 *Ibid.*, p. 4.

66 Williams, *Enhancing Civilian Protection in Peace Operations*, p. 35.

67 'Evaluation of the Implementation and Results of Protection of Civilians Mandates in United Nations Peacekeeping Operations.

68 Martinelli, *The Protection of Civilians During Peacekeeping Operations*, p. 16.

69 Paul Bonard, 'Three Short Proposals to Enhance the Protection of Civilians in Armed Conflict', in Carr Center Working Paper (ed.), *Improving the Protection of Civilians in Situations of Armed Conflict* (Cambridge, MA: Carr Center, May 2011), p. 21.

70 Seth Appiah-Mensah and Rachel Eklou-Assogbavi, 'The Protection of Civilians: A Comparison between United Nations and African Union Peace Operations', *Conflict Trends*, no. 2, 2012, p. 14.

71 *Ibid.*

72 Security Council Report, *Protection of Civilians: Cross Cutting Report: No. 2*, p. 10.

73 Williams, *Enhancing Civilian Protection in Peace Operations*, p. 34.

CONCLUSION

Armed groups are a symptom of conflict, in that they emerge from conditions born of deep-rooted structural problems, such as ethnic dislocation, marginalisation, land issues (including herder–farmer conflicts), economic distortions and historical grievances. As suggested in Chapter One, these problems are the by-products of weak governance and the inability of political-economic systems to effectively mitigate developing conflicts.

It is likely that future conflicts will take place in more crowded, connected and urban environments. Conflicts will continue to be complex, protracted, fragmented, low-intensity and 'fought on the peripheries of states [with armed groups tending] to be militarily weak and factionalized'.[1] On these peripheries, armed groups have, and will continue to exploit weak governance, and take advantage of the opportunities afforded by security vacuums. A picture of regional conflict complexes (such as in West Africa, the Sahel and Central Africa) is also beginning to come into sharper focus. Conflict is layered regional upon national, and national upon regional.

Amidst these conflicts, armed groups evolve while exploring the world of criminal enterprise. In many regions, analysts have reported the existence of a convergence of this form – 'a connection between networks of organised crime, as well as their illicit activities, including money laundering, kidnapping, drug trafficking, terrorism'.[2] It is clear that in the modern era, very few armed groups are revolutionaries riding a wave of popular support. Instead, the armed groups of modern conflict enjoy nominal popular support, and fight on the basis of a mostly self-serving and narrowly defined set of interests – namely power and material wealth. However, as has been argued in Chapter One, the driving motivations of groups are neither constant nor always coherent. Naturally, in unstable and zero-trust environments, groups will remain hyper-vigilant to threats and will jealously guard their base of power for fear of losing out to opportunists. For these groups, committing to a process of any sort (including a disarmament process) represents a compromise or a risk, while continued conflict and instability – the status quo – represents continued opportunity.

This is the operating environment of the new breed of UN missions. The Security Council has habitually placed UN missions into non-permissive environments that resemble more of a pause in conflict than a cessation in hostilities (CAR, Mali, Darfur and DRC). In these environments, UN missions have conducted their business in myriad ways, as highlighted in Chapter Two. Most often, the Security Council has reacted to events on the ground by beefing up respective mandates and sending more troops into the fray. Miscalculations of this nature continually set back missions, and stack the odds against any form of lasting peace and security.

This book has argued that in non-permissive environments, where no negative peace exists, a Chapter VII mandate is a license for a mission to change the facts on the ground – to attempt to create a more permissive environment for negative peace to develop. The key for each UN mission is to calibrate its political and military instruments to suit the context. The political and military components of the mission should be proactive, anticipating potential engagement by spoilers. Under these conditions, the negotiating table and DDR programme should be made as inviting as possible, while at the same time unbearable costs should be attached to continuing civilian victimisation and spoiler activity. If a spoiler continues to pursue violent means for political or economic ends, the spoiler can expect to be robustly countered and pressured into abandoning such means. In this respect, the application of leverage through the means of both political engagement and military deterrence and coercion form the basis of a UN mission's agency.

When the UN encourages political engagement, it should seek to break down inflexibility, build confidence and accommodate reasonable demands. By positioning itself above the parties, the UN can draw on its moral authority, recognising and reporting lax, deferred or stymied implementation of agreements. It has been seen that the most successful missions – ONUMOZ, UNTAG and ONUSAL – are those that focus on political engagement. These missions had successfully inhabited the roles discussed in Chapter Four. Yet, unfortunately, all too often the self-interested winners of the process can effectively capture the state and compete with other national political elites. The problem is that political processes can be usurped by interest groups, resulting in fragile elite pacts designed to divide the spoils of government. An elite pact often amounts to a superficial balancing act, which can unfortunately serve to replicate the exclusive government structures that bore the conflict in the first place – only under a different guise and with a veneer of legitimacy.

The political process should drive the mission, as Chapter Three has made clear, yet too frequently UN missions have failed to avert crises due to a lack of political engagement. Certain missions could even be accused of sleepwalking through the so-called political process, headlong into a crisis. UNMIT in East Timor was one such mission: '…the failure to foresee and attempt to avert the crisis was a consequence of inadequate political engagement, rather than of premature withdrawal of the military component.'[3] As each mission must move a political process forward, the political component must be at the core of the mission. Tackling the root causes of a conflict, rather than allowing conflict to recreate itself under a different guise, is crucial. A political process should incorporate a mix of different methods (top-down and bottom-up) designed to address the diverse roots of conflict while being held together by a coherent strategy. The political core of the mission should be staffed by a strong team, with political-affairs officers working alongside country-specific experts to provide accurate information on context.

The Horta Report

It has been 14 years since the Brahimi Report was published and in that time, the UN has ventured to the Sudans, CAR, Chad, Libya, Nepal, Liberia, Cote d'Ivoire, Mali, has gone back to Haiti, and continued its engagement in the DRC. In late 2014, UN leaders concluded that an update was required to reset the doctrinal project, clarify the grey areas relating to principle and signal a change in the ambitions of peace operations. The secretary-general appointed a panel, chaired by Jose Ramos Horta, to undertake this task. The panel might well consider and address a series of fundamental questions: How can the UN streamline mandates? How can the UN address the problems of template thinking and develop improved context-sensitive approaches? How can the UN improve the interface between military operations and the political process? How do we develop lines of effort to deliver more coordinated and integrated UN operations? How ambitious should UN peace-keeping be? Is the UN overreaching? Should the UN have more limited, realistic goals? How can missions nurture political processes? How can the UN address the gap between expectations and reality in POC?

Two topics are likely to be key considerations for the panel. The first is stabilisation, which first entered common usage in the military following deployment of SFOR to Bosnia in the late 1990s. Since then doctrinal writers in the US and the UK have sought to develop stabilisation doctrines. Although closely associated with counter-insurgency, stabilisation is a distinct approach designed to be 'used in situations of violent conflict…to protect and promote legitimate political authority, using a combination of integrated civilian and military actions to reduce violence, re-establish security and prepare for longer-term recovery'.[4] In the late 2000s, the UN adopted the term and used it to brand several of its missions. For the UN, stabilisation seems to imply support for incumbent administrations or transitional governments. In practice, a UN mission might work closely with the host government, while the mission's military component might conduct joint military operations against an insurgency – the UN effectively acts as fortification for the incumbent government. What if the government in question is pursuing a conflict-creating policy agenda? If the UN were to support a divisive government it would be undermining the very peace it intends to nurture. In short, UN stabilisation missions could be drawn into de facto counter-insurgency campaigns, necessitating the abandonment of the principle of impartiality. Clearly, the UN needs to invest considerable time and energy into a doctrinal project aimed at coming to terms with the implications of stabilisation.

The second issue is the phenomenon of peacekeepers being targeted, in particular with the use of asymmetric methods. During 2014 an alarming number of attacks were launched against UN peacekeepers and 38 were killed. In Mali, for instance, several peacekeepers were killed when a suicide bomb exploded near the checkpoint they were manning.[5] In Darfur and South Sudan, bandits and unidentified armed groups regularly ambushed peacekeepers. It seems that the UN is increasingly being seen by a growing number of armed groups as a soft target. UN missions are not always perceived as impartial, and it is apparent that some groups would relish the opportunity to wage asymmetric campaigns against the UN – with car bombings, IEDs, urban siege or suicide attacks. It is conceivable that, if the UN is eventually deployed in Syria or Somalia, a host of more sophisticated spoilers would be willing to incur significant losses of troops in order to precipitate complete UN withdrawal. Responding to the growing asymmetric threat posed by armed groups, therefore, will require a great deal of thought by the panel.

Mandates and UN relations with TCCs

UN peacekeeping missions should be built around a political core, enabled by strong leadership and supported by an innovative military component. When addressing spoilers, missions should employ creative ways to wedge and constrain armed groups – cutting off their access to weapons and funding, for example – as well as directly confronting them through the use of force.

As argued in Chapter Four, TCCs are questioning what robust peacekeeping is. This *Adelphi* has attempted to further develop the concept and remove some of the ambiguities surrounding it. More work must be done. Ties between the TCCs, the Security Council and financial contributors should be strengthened, so that a single unified concept of peacekeeping is promoted. For now, a shared understanding has yet to be built among member states 'on the nature and scope of robust peacekeeping, and the specific command and control arrangements that its successful implementation requires'.[6]

If it is decided that such a consensus cannot be reached, member states should seek to outline the possible alternatives to robust peacekeeping in non-permissive environments. There are several options the UN could pursue. Firstly, peacekeeping could fall back on a passive Chapter VI style of operation, which would only allow peacekeepers to ameliorate the situation and defend themselves against attacks. However, this approach does not account for the changing nature of conflict today. Secondly, the UN could strip missions of their military components, in an effort to focus entirely on the political solution. Thus, UN missions in difficult circumstances would become Special Political Missions (SPMs). This option is also not viable, as many situations require the deployment of troops to restore the security situation, before peacebuilding can begin. Thirdly, the mandating of so-called 'super robust' or peace-enforcement operations could occur. This option, however, would create two groups of peacekeepers: those willing to use force beyond self-defence and those that would not.

A key challenge is the risk- and burden-sharing gap, which limits the troop contributions available for robust peacekeeping. At present, countries of the Global South provide the bulk of peacekeepers, and in so doing, shoulder risks inherent to robust peacekeeping. The countries of the Global North, by comparison, contribute a mere 5% of the total number of UN peacekeepers. This should be increased, in order to 'give these governments a direct stake in a particular operation; which is more than simply voting 'yes' in the Security Council or providing funding through the peacekeeping budget'.[7] It is clear that 'the political leverage applied by more representative and strengthened peacekeeping operations would be greater'.[8] The best way forward is to gradually convince the TCCs that a proactive robust approach is the most effective one. The leadership must also bring the various stakeholders together and forge a new compact for peacekeeping. It is hoped that this book will stimulate the necessary conversation on developing the concept of robust peacekeeping.

The UN needs to develop mechanisms to empower peace processes and tackle those parties that continually seek to undermine the peace. The Security Council's use of panel of experts has proven useful in certain circumstances – Angola, for instance. Yet, the six-month reporting mechanisms usually only confirm suspicions, with panel reports merely naming and shaming sanctions violators. Those that are named and shamed often then attack the credibility of the findings or refute the reliability of the panel's methodologies, weakening their effectiveness. Likewise, sanctions are not tight enough to suffocate a spoiler and induce a change in behaviour.

In non-permissive environments, UN missions should explore the possibilities of establishing an interdiction task force (potentially linked to an in-mission sanctions-monitoring unit) charged with investigating the logistical and financial flows made available to spoilers or potential spoilers. In other words, follow the money and guns. Once enough evidence has been collected, the mission can then manoeuvre to interdict logistics chains. When a spoiler's financial base shrinks and their military capacity is degraded, they will be more likely to heed demands than if they were subject to Security Council sanctions. The JMAC (the analytical hub of the mission) can also be used more instrumentally to profile spoilers and understand their logistics chains. This information can then be used to empower interdiction operations aimed at choking targeted spoilers.

Reforming the UN system

The management and backstopping of peace operations is undertaken by the DPKO for peacekeeping missions, and by the Department of Political Affairs (DPA) for special political missions. As currently constituted, many SPMs are essentially peacekeeping missions without a military component. At the same time, these missions also often struggle with the political dimension of their mandates. In order to strengthen the UN's work in field operations, therefore, Ian Martin has suggested that the UN merge the DPA, the DPKO, and the Peacebuilding Support Office (PBSO) to create a new overarching department called the Department of Peace and Security.

Such a move would seek the 'modification of UN departmental structures, funding mechanisms and mandating and accountability arrangements, with the objective of creating a system able to ensure that field operations are designed, modified, funded and managed according to the mix of political, peacekeeping and peacebuilding functions required by each country context and its evolution'.[9] The reform would erase the false distinction made between DPA and DPKO. In so doing, the merger would strengthen the availability of political and mediation resources for peacekeeping, while also providing SPMs with dependable funding ensured through the assessed peacekeeping budget. The UN also needs to do a better job of ensuring that it has the right personnel in place to take advantage of a new consensus around robust peacekeeping and increased support from the most militarily advanced states. As the UK's permanent representative to the UN has observed:

> You can have 20,000 troops, you can have 5,000 troops, it doesn't make a blind bit of difference if they are not properly led ... guided and directed by the leadership ... it's absolutely critical that the Secretary-General

appoints the right people as SRSGs.[10]

The SRSG is the designated UN official and head of mission in country. As UN missions are managed under a decentralised leadership structure, the SRSG, acting as the head of mission, is vested with a high degree of discretionary power. This structure places a premium on the quality of leadership at the mission level. Ian Martin succinctly describes the role of the SRSG:

> The key responsibility of the SRSG is to set a clear strategy for the mission, to make sure that everyone understands it and is on board with it and that the different components of the mission cooperate in carrying out that strategy – rather than fight each other to pursue contradictory goals or even the same goal in contradictory or competitive ways. That's really the SRSG's job, but you are up against big cultural conflicts, between the military, police, electoral, and civilian public information types.[11]

Unfortunately, the UN has consistently failed to appoint competent people to the position of SRSG, and although, 'the UN secretariat has invested heavily in senior leadership training in recent years ... [many senior UN officials] admit that mission leaders are often chosen for political rather than meritocratic reasons'.[12] The skill sets and competence of SRSGs vary considerably, as there exists neither a standardised competency-based recruitment process nor a comprehensive training course for SRSGs prior to their deployment.

As indicated, there exists a void at the UN in terms of leadership development. The Secretariat should build a rigorous competency-based selection mechanism, as well as an in-house leadership-development programme aimed at identifying potential mission leaders (the next Sergio Vieira de Mello) from within the UN system. Surveying the current cadre of SRSGs, few have UN mission experience, and many are former diplomats and politicians. There needs to be recognition that not all skill sets are directly transferable. Indeed, the role of the SRSG requires a very diverse and particular set of skills – administrative, management, process facilitation, mediation and civil–military coordination.[13] Only those that possess the appropriate combination of knowledge and skills should be selected to join the organisational leadership.

Tailoring missions

Knowing that a force deployed into a non-permissive environment is likely to encounter spoilers, the force-generation process should account for this. With so few troops available, peacekeeping needs to be innovative – as creativity has arguably the greatest force-multiplier effect. The key is a tailor-made force, designed specifically for the job at hand. If a situation warrants fewer infantry and more special forces, the OMA should seek to generate a force with such a composition. The current reliance on static posture also needs to change. Peacekeepers need to move out from their bases and into the community, and into remote areas. Patrol bases or mobile operating bases can greatly improve a force's ability to protect civilians, as peacekeepers are living amongst the communities they are charged with protecting. In the mid-2000s, MONUC championed this style of operation in Democratic Republic of the Congo (DCR). However, many TCCs and the General Assembly have insisted on promoting a form of force protection that relies on fortified bases.

Since the UN entered into the realm of multidimensional peacekeeping in the early 1990s, missions in many theatres have had to come to terms with operating in parallel with other foreign forces. In Bosnia, the UN after 1993 could call upon NATO close-air support under the infamous dual-key system. In Somalia, UNOSOM II operated alongside US Task Force Ranger, a detachment of Deltas and Rangers stationed at Mogadishu airport. In both cases, complications arose from conducting military operations simultaneously under separate command structures in the same theatre. The challenges of multinational command are immense, but they are multiplied when another military operation is operating in-theatre simultaneously. The problem manifests itself most pointedly at times of crisis, when commanders act at cross purposes on the basis of divergent reasoning or irreconcilable objectives.

The UN blue force and green force (parallel mission) should avoid these arrangements unless some benefit can be derived. The case of CAR represents a cautionary tale; a patchwork of so-called peacekeepers from the African Union (MISCA), France and later the EU deployed in the capital Bangui and elsewhere in an effort to curb the violence without a cohesive stabilisation strategy. French forces began to disarm Séléka fighters in Bangui, but by 'doing so, they created a power vacuum, which enabled Christian militias, the anti-Balaka, to attack the city's Muslim minority unhindered'.[14] They became part of the problem. Chadian troops, on the other hand, supported Séléka and Muslim communities.

Yet, the reality of the matter is that UN missions will continue to work in partnership with other military forces, in the same theatre. For this arrangement to work, however, both forces (UN mission and parallel force) 'should be joined at the hip'.[15] If command structures are not integrated, commanders of both the blue and green forces must devise mechanisms designed to engender synergy and aid in the conduct of joint operations. It has been shown in places such as Sierra Leone[16] that blue and green forces can operate effectively in tandem to create a 'good cop' (blue force), 'bad cop' (green force) dynamic.[17]

Strong analysis should back the political core of each UN mission. In fact, the entire mission should be shaped by a close reading of the environment – an understanding of the facts on the ground. Intelligence and analysis are absolutely critical to the successful persecution of peacekeeping operations. If missions are better able to understand their environments, they will be better able to craft effective strategies to achieve sustainable outcomes. Enhanced understanding of the local context helps to repair the conflict-management structures and processes inherent to each community, within the area of deployment. To understand a peacekeeping environment there is a need to model the complex human, physical and informational terrain within the area of deployment. Analysis should not be compartmentalised within a mission structure. Instead, it should form the basis of the decision-making processes of senior leadership and field staff alike. In simple terms, analysis should be folded into the political and military projects of the mission, and used to anticipate ruptures in the fabric of the peace process.

In accompaniment to the conflict analysis suggested above, UN missions should attempt to undertake armed-group profiling and cartography. (A good guide to armed-group profiling is the fine-grained analysis practised by Jason Stearns and his team at the Rift Valley Institute's Usalama Project.[18]) Missions must not only comprehend the armed groups themselves – leadership, motivation, popular support, logistics and structure – but also the ties between various other actors in the complex environments they inhabit. Profiling and link analysis should be undertaken with an appreciation of the political, ethno-religious, social, historical and regional dynamics that make each context unique. There are a range of new tools which can aid this type of detailed field analysis, including Open Street Map (OSM),[19] heat mapping, link analysis (using i2 intelligence software) and GIS analysis. Cheap, readily applicable technology tools provide myriad possibilities that the UN should take advantage of.

Technology, however, is not the cure-all. Recently there has been a focus on surveillance drones in support of MONUSCO in the DRC. Drones are certainly useful, but they cannot be used as a substitute for strong human-intelligence sources and hard-core analysis. The invention of both the Joint Mission Analysis Centre (JMAC) and the Joint Operation Centre (JOC) in 2004 began the job of closing the gap in situational-awareness terms. Nevertheless, more is required. The UN has huge information-gathering potential it should tap into – from the peacekeeper on foot patrol to field workers in disparate and remote locations to open-source information freely available (on social media, crowd-sourcing, blogs and news sources, for example). The hard part is then making use of the information effectively to help decision-makers.

Ralph J. Bunche once said that the 'United Nations exists not merely to preserve the peace but also to make change – even radical change ... the United Nations has no vested interest in the status quo. It seeks a more secure world, a better world, a world of progress for all peoples.' This captures the spirit that should define the heart of every peacekeeping mission: courage, perceptiveness and creativity. The UN must carry these virtues into the field to effect change, not stand by idly as peace is undermined or a settlement exploited by spoilers. It has long followed the first part of Theodore Roosevelt's maxim, 'speak softly and carry a big stick', by engaging politically and cajoling parties to negotiate. The time is overdue for this to be complemented by credible force.

Notes

1   Jakkie Cilliers and Julia Schuene-mann, 'The Future of Intrastate Conflict in Africa: More Violence or Greater Peace?' Institute of Security Studies Paper no. 246, 15 May 2013, p. 4.

2   *Ibid.*

3   *Ibid.*

4   'The UK Government's Approach to Stabilisation', *FCO, MOD, DFID and Stabilisation* (London: UK Government, 2014), p. 1.

5   'UN Peacekeepers Killed in Northern Mali', Al Jazeera, 14 December 2013, http://www. aljazeera.com/news/africa/2013/12/ un-peacekeepers-killed-northern-mali-2013121492252314392.html.

6   Jean-Marie Guéhenno, 'Robust Peacekeeping: Building Political Consensus and Strengthening Command and Control', in NYC Center for International Cooperation (ed.), *Robust Peacekeeping: The Politics of Force* (New York: NYC CIC, 2009), p. 11.

7   See Peter Nadin, 'After Afghanistan: A Return to UN Peacekeeping?', Our World, 5 March 2014, http:// unu.edu/publications/articles/ after-afghanistan-a-return-to-un-peacekeeping.html.

8   *Ibid.*

9   See Ian Martin, 'All Peace Operations Are Political: A Case for Designer Missions and the Next UN Reform', in NYC Center for International Cooperation (ed.), *Review of Political Missions 2010*, http://cic.nyu.edu/ sites/default/files/political_missions _2010_martin_allpeace2.pdf.

10 See 'UN Peacekeeping on Blue Helmets: New Frontiers – High Level Seminar', quote by Mark Lyall Grant, 19 December 2013, http://webtv.un.org/search/ un-peacekeeping-on-blue-helmets-new-frontiers-high-level-seminar/2 955323973001?term=peacekeeping .

11 Sukehiro Hasegawa, 'UN Peace Mission Leadership: Achieving Unity of Efforts', *ACUNS Quarterly Newsletter*, no. 4, 2012, p. 4, citing Connie Peck, *On Being a Special Representative of the Secretary General* (Geneva: UNITAR, 2006), p. 116.

12 Richard Gowan and Bruce Jones, 'Leadership and the Use of Force in Peace Operations', in *Annual Review of Global Peace Operations 2013* (New York: Lynne Rienner, 2013), pp. 24–5.

13 Assistant secretaries-general, under secretaries-general, directors and chiefs in New York also often have challenging relationships with respective SRSGs. The attitude of certain SRSGs has been one of arro-gance, rather than humility; 'the SRSG will see the secretary-general only if God is unavailable'. Author interview with Ian Martin, 2013.

14 Max Borowski, 'French Troops Fail to Stop the Violence in CAR', Deutsche Welle, 9 January 2014, http://www.dw.de/french-troops-fail-to-stop-the-violence-in-car/a-17351664.

15 Interview with Jean-Marie Guéhenno, 2013.

16 In Sierra Leone: UNAMSIL (blue force) and the United Kingdom's *Operation Palliser* (green force).

17 US Army Peacekeeping and Stability Operations Institute (PKSOI), 'Strategic Lesson Number 19: "Blue" and "Green" Forces

Operating in Tandem' (Carlisle, PA: PKSOI, 2013).

18 See examples of armed-group profiling at http://www.riftvalley.net/key-projects/usalama.

19 See examples of conflict mapping at http://www.thedailybeast.com/articles/2014/03/10/aleppo-conflict-map-shows-assad-s-control-by-neighborhood.html.

Table 1.1: **A typology of armed groups**

Identity	Definition
Rebels	An all-encompassing term for a group that 'rises in opposition or armed resistance against an established government or leader'.
Militia	Traditionally militia groups comprised citizen-soldiers, who could be called upon to serve the community at a time of emergency. Contemporary militias are much harder to define; but drawing on the traditional concept, militias can be appropriately defined as communal self-defence groups, whose aim is to protect the citizenry of a particular community, as well as their way of life (property, territory and laws).
Guerrilla	An armed insurrectionist group, which acts as the 'foco' for popular and general insurrection. The guerrilla epitomises asymmetrical warfare, as Mao suggested: 'when guerrillas engage a stronger enemy, they withdraw when he advances; harass him when he stops; strike him when he is weary; pursue him when he withdraws'. [1] Guerrilla groups are characterised as small, highly mobile cadres (exploiting the weaknesses of traditional armies). They employ classic asymmetrical tactics: ambushes, raids, hit-and-run and sabotage.
Insurgent	A term which has re-entered military parlance following the invasions of Afghanistan and Iraq. In both countries, 'the insurgent' quickly emerged as the enemy of occupying forces. In the classic sense, an 'insurgency is a struggle to control a contested political space, between a state (or group of states or occupying powers), and one or more popularly based, non-state challengers'. [2] In a modern context, insurgents might not actually seek to overthrow the state (in Iraq insurgents were attempting to destroy the state rather than supplant it), and may not even pursue a coherent strategy.
Revolutionary	A group which aims to 'turn around' (in Latin) the established order. An armed revolutionary seeks radical change of the political, economic and/or social order, which usually involves the transformation of the state and a change of government. Revolutionaries strive to supplant the dominant governing ideologies and replace them with their brand: communism, socialism, fascism, nationalism, republicanism and liberalism. Counter-revolutionaries (reactionaries), on the other hand, favour the status quo and react violently against revolution, in support of the established order.
Separatists	A group which seeks the separation of a people (ethnic, tribal, religious) from a larger entity – usually the state. Separatists might advocate for secession or greater autonomy within the state.

Table 1.1: **A typology of armed groups**

Warlords	A group which combines both military and civil means to extend their authority over territory (so-called ungoverned spaces) outside of government control, with the aim of extracting an economic benefit. Usually warlords, as conflict entrepreneurs, adopt a 'neofeudal posture to the state, seeking neither to replace nor secede from it, but rather to exercise a high degree of autonomy'.[3]
Social Bandits	A term coined by historian Eric Hobsbawm; defined as 'peasant outlaws whom the lord and state regard as criminals, but who remain within peasant society, and are considered by their people as heroes, as champions, avengers, fighters for justice, perhaps even leaders of liberation, and in any case as men to be admired, helped and supported'.[4]
Bandits	'One who is proscribed or outlawed; hence, a lawless desperate marauder, a brigand: usually applied to members of the organized gangs.' The notorious 'zaraguinas' (road cutters) of the tormented triangle of northeastern Central African Republic are the archetypal contemporary bandits. The road cutters exploit ungoverned space, and engage in exploitative activities – robbing, roadblocks, poaching, etc.
State-Surrogate Groups (or Hybrid Groups)	The implicit hand of the state manifests in the form of an armed group. These groups should not be confused with regular military, police or even paramilitary units. Although they might include regular soldiers among their ranks, they are structurally separate from a state's security forces, often for reasons of plausible deniability. For instance, the death squads (or Escuadrón de la Muerte) that operated in El Salvador during the civil war regularly carried out extra-judicial killings on behalf of the government, but were not part of the security services. The degree of separation depends on the context – from wholly own subsidiaries of national governments to limited material, training or funding support.

Notes

1. Mao Tse-tung, *On Guerrilla Warfare* (Champaign, IL: University of Illinois, 1961), p. 46.
2. David Kilcullen, 'Counterinsurgency Redux', *Survival*, vol. 48, no. 4, November 2006, p. 112.
3. James Cockayne, 'Chasing Shadows: Strategic Responses to Organised Crime in Conflict-Affected Situations', *RUSI Journal*, vol. 158, no. 2, April/May 2013, p. 15.
4. Eric Hobsbawn, *Bandits* (London: Weidenfeld & Nicolson, 2000), p. 20.

INDEX